SISTERS, BROTHERS, AND OTHERS

SISTERS, BROTHERS, AND OTHERS

by Suzanne Szasz
and Elizabeth Taleporos, Ph.D.

Photographed by Suzanne Szasz
Foreword by Dr. Benjamin Spock

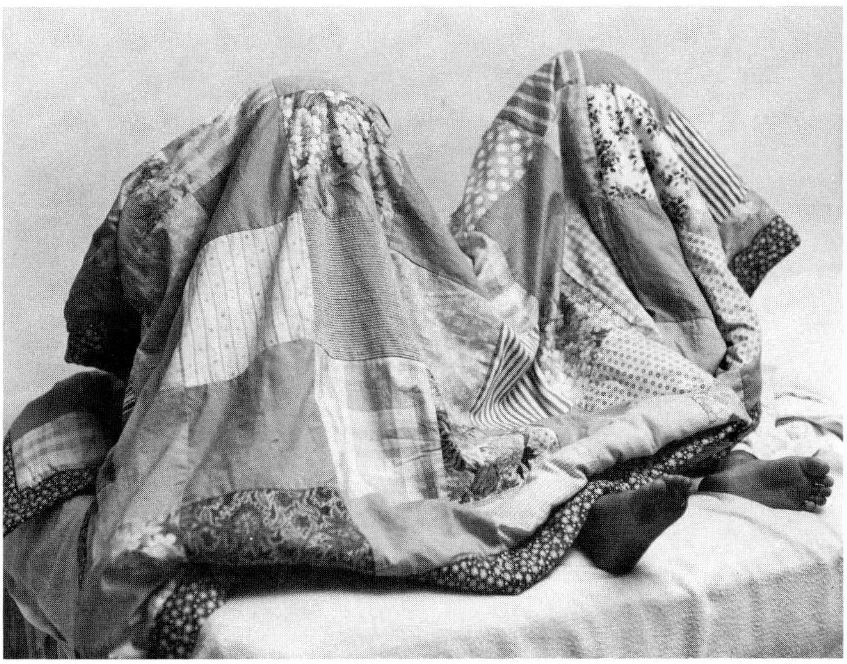

W. W. NORTON & COMPANY
NEW YORK   LONDON

Published simultaneously in Canada by George J. McLeod Limited, Toronto.
Printed in the United States of America.

The text of this book is composed in Goudy Old Style, with
display type set in Goudy Bold. Composition by The Vail-Ballou Press, Inc.
Manufacturing by The Murray Printing Company
Book design by Hermann Strohbach

First Edition

Library of Congress Cataloging in Publication Data
Szasz, Suzanne.
Sisters, brothers, and others.
1. Brothers and sisters. 2. Children—Family relationships.
I. Taleporos, Elizabeth. II. Title.
BF723.S43S92 1984 155.4'43 83-19470

ISBN 0-393-01810-5

W.W. Norton & Company, Inc., 500 Fifth Avenue, New York, N.Y. 10110
W.W. Norton & Company Ltd., 37 Great Russell Street, London WC1B 3NU

1 2 3 4 5 6 7 8 9 0

CONTENTS

We would like to thank several people
who have helped with different aspects of this book.

James Mairs, our editor, for his belief in the value of this book and the work he put into it;
Hermann Strohbach, for his patience in designing a setting to bring out the best in the photographs;
Peter Schults, for his enthusiasm and guidance;
and last but not least,
The Children and their Parents who are the subjects and the reason of this book: thank you for letting us show your feelings and stories!

FOREWORD

BY DR. BENJAMIN SPOCK

This book about siblings should be an eye opener to parents, both new and experienced. It reveals the intensity of children's interactions with each other and with their parents—jealous, joyful, resentful, nurturing, furious, hilarious, loving. You suddenly realize that your own children's attitudes toward life are being shaped right under your nose—this morning, this afternoon, and tonight. As a parent you are one of the principle actors, at center stage. And yet you realize, as I did, that most of the time you haven't been paying enough attention to the important things as they happen. You've been too preoccupied with pressing practicalities—patching up the fights, keeping the food from burning, answering the phone.

To me the unspoken message of this book is to keep your eyes and heart open to the high drama around you so that you can be sensitive to your children's needs and can get the maximum enjoyment from being with them. Soon—too soon—they'll be grown and gone.

There are a number of things about the pictures and text of this book that are impressive to me. The authors know children's emotional development at different ages and the sources of their stresses. They have captured a wide range of siblings' responses in a way that is both exciting and gently instructive. And the most magical thing about Suzanne Szasz's pictures is that Suzanne is invisible in them. I mean that the children are acting in such an utterly natural way—whether joyous or angry or loving—that it never occurs to you that an adult must be there right in their midst.

Suzanne is highly sensitive to the children's moods so that she gets advance warning about what is about to happen and is ready to catch it. She has respect for children in the sense that she's content to be passive and let them be themselves—she doesn't try to arrange them or motivate them, as most of us have the itch to do, especially when we hold a camera. She is self-effacing—she fades into the background so that the children totally forget she is there. By contrast most adults, through lifelong training in politeness, have a compulsion to fill in any silences with cordial talk, thereby calling attention to themselves and distracting children from their natural activities and expressions. Most impressive of all is Suzanne's patience. It must have taken hours of waiting to catch some of the dramatic moments in this book.

Each reader will have her or his favorite pictures. Here are some of mine: the miserable four year old who has stuffed himself into the corner of the sofa and covered his eyes to try to shut out the sight of the new baby being fed by his mother; the grumpy four year old looking abandoned and bitter while his older brother holds the new baby (this is the fate of the middle child: never to be able to catch up to the first, then to lose the particular advantages of being the baby); the two year old standing on the bed, swigging from the bottle while watching, out of the corner of her eye, her mother adoring the baby; saucy Minty trying to distract her mother from the baby—and punish her inattention—by emptying her handbag; Kerry appearing as mature and understanding as a grown woman when she comforts Kathy, though she is only ten; Laura teaching Claire how to draw, a touching picture of pure sisterly love; three delicious sisters giggling; four-year-old Joelle feeling left out of the nursing situation; Tad smiling meanly while his small sister screams with frustration because he won't give her what she wants. They all tell us something about children and about ourselves.

Eleanor and her two children after the birth of Austene and fourteen years later.

INTRODUCTION

We all know how much our parents influence our lives, but we often ignore or forget how vital a part our sisters and brothers play. It is not only an important relationship, but it is also likely to go through many phases.

Three-year-old Peter is a fear-inspiring giant to his infant sister Mary. But in a few months he discovers that the baby sister he hated for commanding so much of his parents' attention is turning into a cute playmate; he likes to boss her around and enjoys being the leader in their games. Soon he is off to school, and the three-year difference in their ages once again seems great. But in a few more years Mary will catch up with Peter again; his friends now like her, and Mary and Peter enjoy doing many of the same things. Suddenly they are both teenagers. If they are lucky, the usual stormy encounters will not be too numerous—and, anyway, they both know by now that their relationship will weather almost anything.

This is just one of the countless scenarios between siblings. Others include sisters whose intense jealousy of each other makes one of them an embittered woman; the other, who always tried to outshine her younger sister, accumulates success upon success at any cost. There are girls so cherished by an older brother that they bring cooperation and admiration into their marriages, and others so used to scrapping with a male sibling that they cannot avoid fighting with their lovers or husbands. In families with several children there are secret wars, pacts, and enduring alliances. Often they continue into adulthood. Recognizing their origin in childhood can be a shock but also instructive.

The nursery seems to be the proving ground of both positive and negative feelings, where sisters and brothers form many of the attitudes that they will show to others later in life.

All parents want their children to get along, to love each other, or at least not to hate each other. Some parents plan to have their children in rapid succession, hoping that their close age will help them grow up as friends. Other parents plan to put two, three, or four years between their children's birthdays, expecting that the older one will have enjoyed his or her share of parental attention and care before there is another baby in the house. Of course, some births are not planned, and parents end up having to deal with children as closely spaced as ten months or as widely spaced as twelve or more years.

Parents often wonder whether they should interfere with their children's relationships. Should they stop a fight? Should they insist that the children share? Will the first child suffer if they have a second one? Will they have enough love for all? Can they afford to have another child? And, most importantly, how can they insure that love and intimacy prevail in their children's life?

The answers to these and a hundred related questions are as varied as the people who struggle with the problems. There are no "right" and "wrong" answers most of the time. Everyone has to work out his or her own solutions. In this book we have shown many different problems and how some people have dealt with them. Perhaps you will recognize your own children in them.

Chris and Pegge, overcome with laughter on an excursion when they were four and six years old; and now, at age twenty-seven and twenty-nine, still friends.

Neither I nor Gini can interpret her forlorn expression at the age of five, when her one-year-old sister Gaye tries to climb into her lap. Grown up, they love each other enthusiastically and consider themselves best friends.

NEW BABY

Contrary to popular myth, love is rarely instant. Newborns are strangers to their brothers and sisters. To make things worse, they are rarely attractive. The delivery process often produces pointed heads and bruises. Many newborns develop a yellowish hue to their skin from normal newborn jaundice. The umbilical cord is unappealing. And the behavior of newborns rarely engenders love. They cry a lot. They don't play. They sleep a great deal, and when they are up they need a lot of fussing; they are incredibly messy.

All this is quite a disappointment for sisters and brothers who have been led to expect nothing less than a cute diaper-ad baby, smiling and gurgling at them. And, to make things worse, adults all around seem to be saying things like "Isn't she cute? Don't you just love your baby sister?" Then they proceed to shower gifts on this undeveloped person who can hardly appreciate the presents and the attention half as much as they, the walking, talking, loving older child.

Fortunately, things get better. As the baby acquires a personality, the household settles down and adjusts. Eventually, things work out so that everyone's needs are met in some fashion, even if the baby still gets the lion's share of attention. In a few months, the newborn begins to react with a range of emotion. The first smile is often provoked by an older sibling. The baby begins to look cute, to smile and laugh. In five or six months, the baby has become a person, who can sit up, play, and enjoy his brother or sister.

The birth of a baby is always a time for heightened emotions in a family. Setting a positive tone in these early months can help pave the way for a positive relationship between the siblings—although it cannot ensure it.

There are many ways in which parents can help older children understand the ways of babies. They have to be told, first of all, that babies are not toys and need careful handling. Parents also need to be around to teach the children to play together in a way that is fun but does not become unsafe. It is not only the babies who need protection: even small babies love to pull hair, grab, or bite fingers in ways that can frighten and hurt unsuspecting older children. They, in turn, may misjudge babies' need for support and let go suddenly, or express their ambivalent feelings by playing rough.

It is a thin line that separates being overprotective from too relaxed, and all parents recognize it sooner or later.

Elizabeth was 5 years old when her mother told her of the new baby. She had been the youngest for all these years. Would she be upset to cede this position to a newcomer? Or would it be nice to have someone else be the youngest and get blamed by the others?

Curiosity

For most children, the new baby is an object of curiosity. They are fascinated by the miniature person; they like to compare their hands to the baby's and see how much bigger they are. Most are also fascinated by the baby's genitals, especially when the baby is of the opposite sex. Many parents encourage the older siblings to participate in family routines like bath time and diaper change so that the need to see and compare themselves to the baby is easily met.

Howard was four and Chris two when their sister Pegge was born. Their main emotion seemed to be curiosity about everything concerning the new arrival. They spent much time watching her and asking questions about her.

On the day that his parents brought his new baby sister home, four-year-old Morgan was full of curiosity. His mother let him see her being bathed and fed, burped and cuddled. He kept asking his mother questions, and he kept eating crackers. He was glad that the baby slept so much that his mother had time to be with him alone many times during the day.

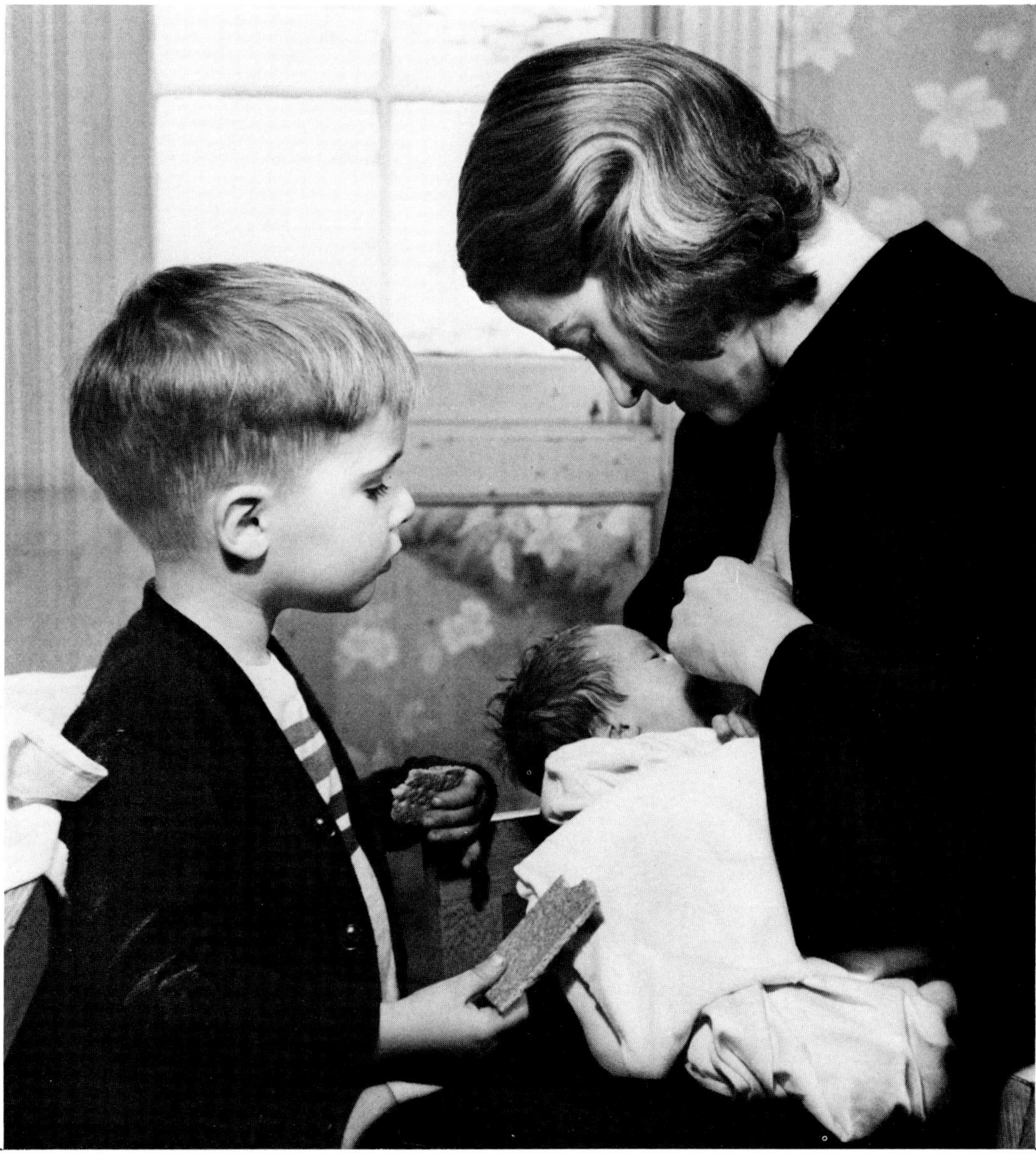

There is something irresistible about a baby's feet that are peeking out from under a blanket. Minty, three, smiles delightedly as she holds them.

Andrew likes to get up early in the morning and pay his six-month-old sister a visit and entertain her. From the next room, his parents listen carefully to catch the first signs of possible trouble.

Early Interactions

Early interactions between siblings can influence later relationships. Few parents would bring home a new baby nowadays without ever having mentioned and explained the mother's pregnancy, then proceed to change the older child's living arrangements without asking her opinion, and then ignore all her confusion and hostility by insisting that she felt nothing but love for the little one. Yet for one of us (Suzanne) "this is what I remember of my sister's arrival at age four. I am relieved that my subsequent attempts to hurt the baby were unsuccessful and that—much later—we became loving friends. But there is nothing that influenced my life more than trying to suppress my hurt and jealousy and to win my parents' love by any means: being a "model" child, always compliant—but always angry underneath, of course."

Three-year-old Billy has asked to be allowed to hold his little brother Nat. He is careful to support his head, but the baby seems much bigger and heavier than he thought. He is quite relieved when he can return the baby to his mother.

Learning to Live with a Baby

Before a second child is born, the first-born is used to being the center of the parents' attention. They might have had other interests, too, but all child-related concern belonged to him or her. With the arrival of the new baby, this role changes; the older is still part of the family, but not the only one. Each day brings new adjustments and the necessity to surrender or share the focus of attention at times.

Many older children become very jealous of the newborn and attempt to draw attention to themselves in many ways. Some of these attempts are negative—provoking fights, regressing to earlier behavior—and some are positive—getting good grades in school to please a favorite teacher.

Parents find it hard to cope with these maneuvers, as the children choose just the moments when their demands are hardest to satisfy. Older brother needs a drink at the same instant that Mother is starting to feed the baby; the toy that was delighting older sister just before the baby needed changing breaks mysteriously.

Some parents anticipate and are ready to fulfill these requests. Others give children a baby of their own to fuss over regardless of whether they are girls or boys and make quite a production about calling them away from play because their dollbaby needs to be fed or changed.

Billy, seven, who has had to live with his jealousy of his four-year-old brother Robert in past years, now gets back at him by emphasizing his privileges with the baby. He is excluding his younger brother by the way he is holding the baby away from him. Every new child creates new alliances and constellations in a family.

Four-year-old Chris got out of bed when he heard his mother move around in the kitchen. Now he is patiently waiting until the baby finishes his bottle, so he can have breakfast, too. Patience is one of the hard things to learn when a new baby needs so much of the parents' time. And, seeing the baby's numerous feedings, some children get jealous of the food itself.

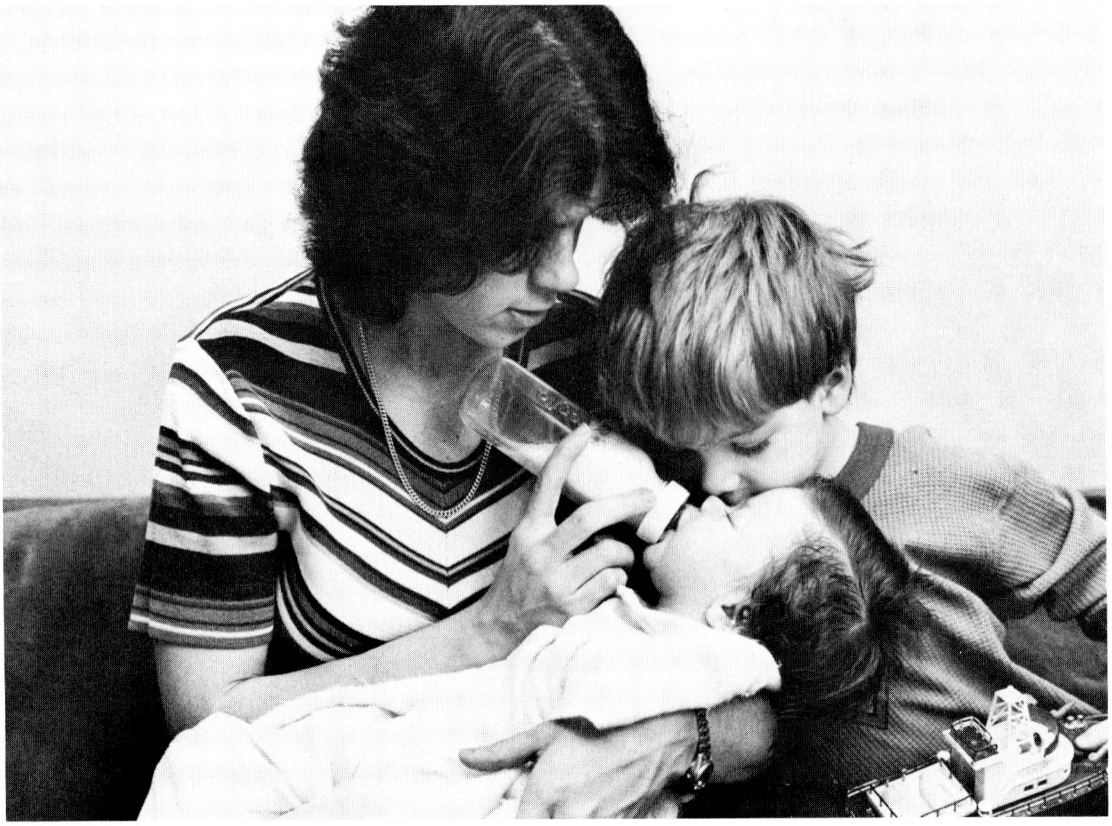

Jealousy

As his mother starts to feed three-week-old baby Kerri, four-year-old Kevin nestles close to both of them, enjoying kissing the baby.

But the feeding seems to be going on too long; Kevin would like to play at something else now. His mother's patient explanations are of no avail: he is getting angry. He would like his mother's undivided attention again. Why did she have to bring home this new baby anyway?

Finally, Kevin curls up on the sofa, trying to shut out the world. Maybe it would not be such a bad idea to go to nursery school again, he thinks.

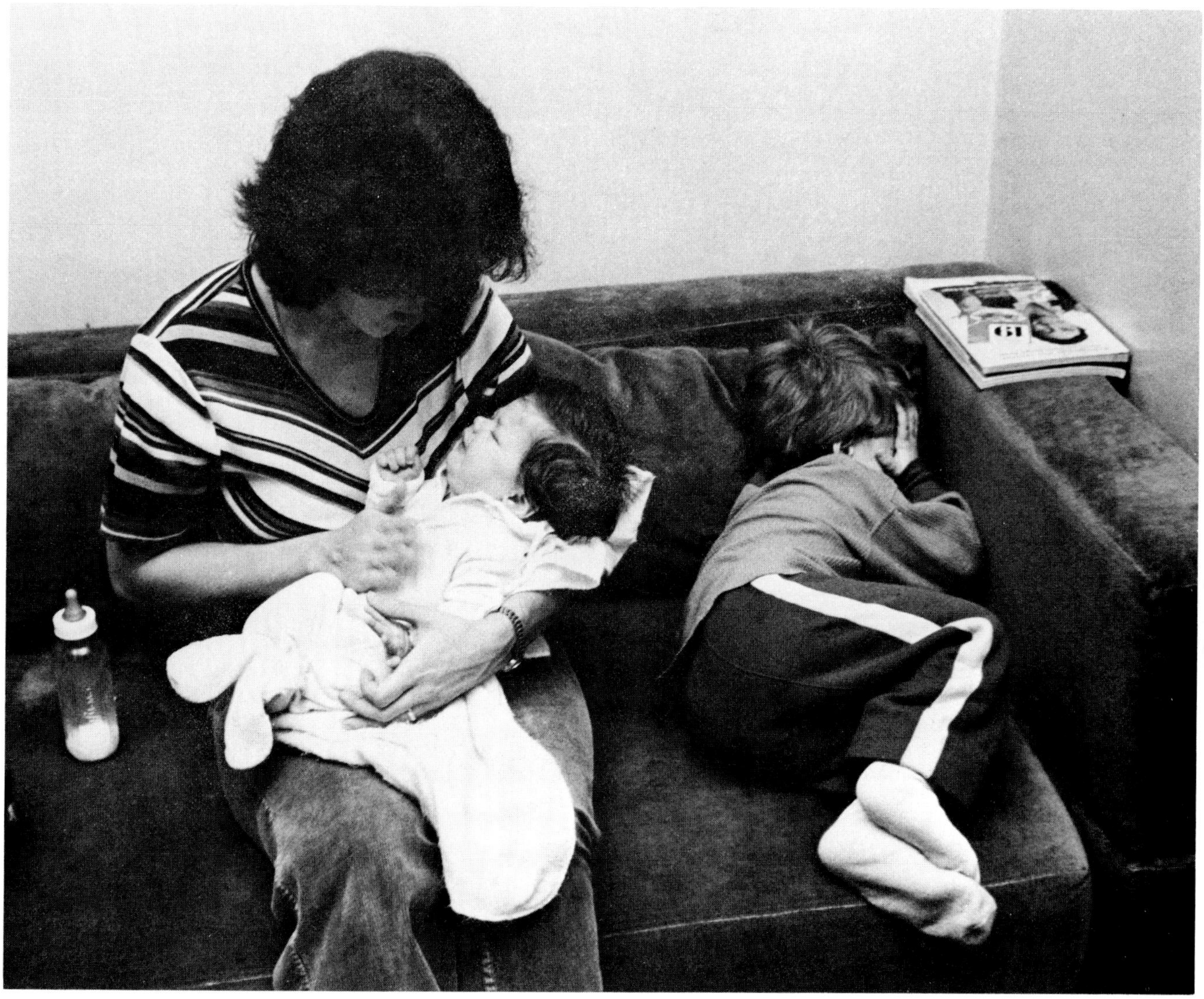

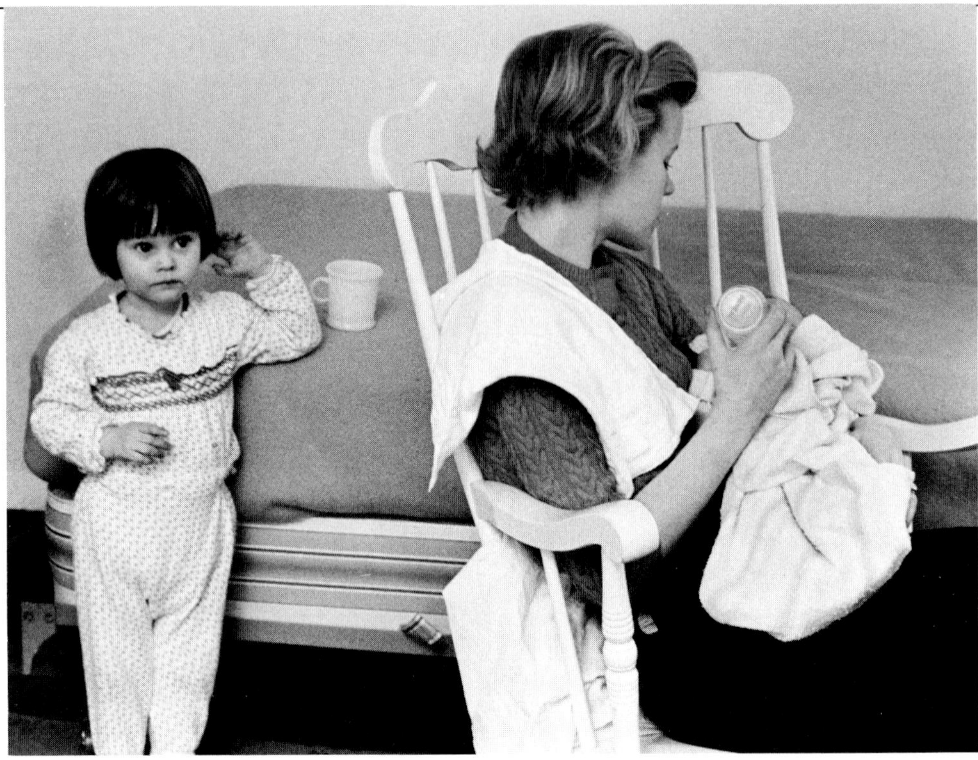

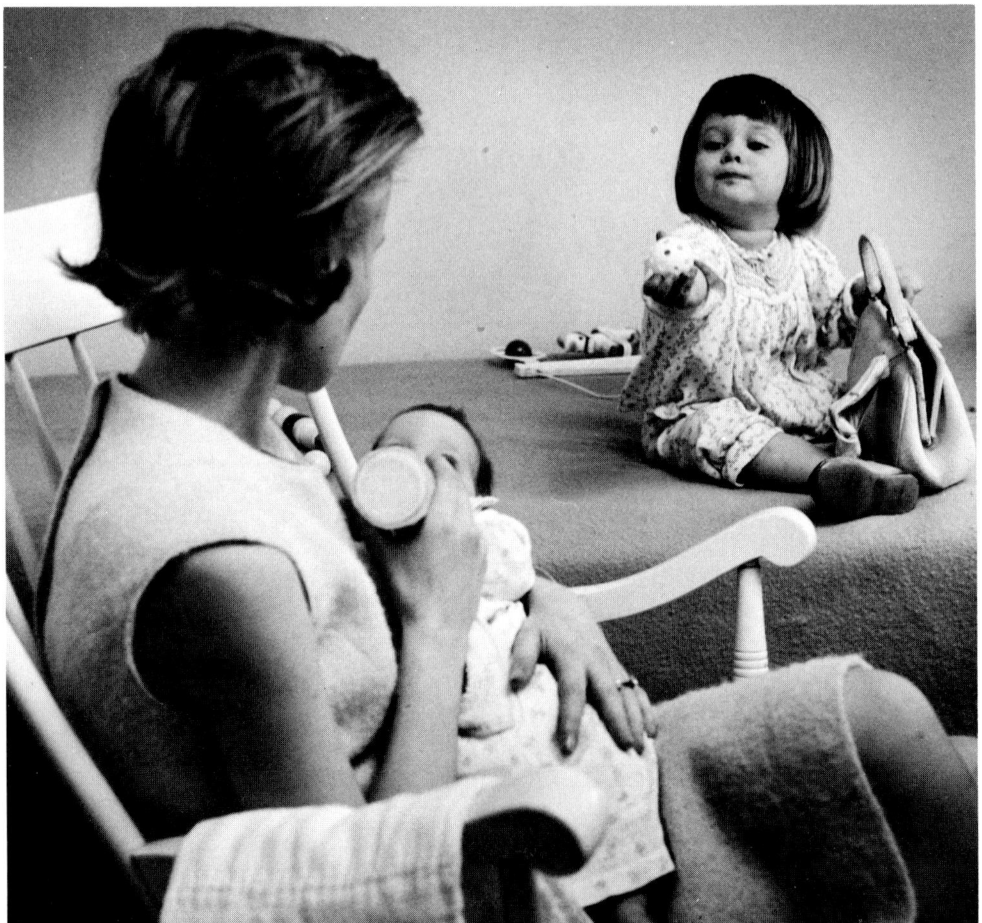

Competing with a Baby

Mother is feeding the baby. Behind her back, three-year-old Minty watches wistfully. Many mothers have commented upon seeing similar photographs that they never knew what their older child felt when they were occupied with the baby.

For a three year old, the time that it takes a baby to finish a bottle seems endless. After a while, Minty changes her tactics; she climbs up on the sofa and proceeds to empty her mother's handbag, hoping to distract her from her involvement with the baby.

Daddy is playing with four-month-old Melissa. Their joyful noise brings Minty running: she wants to participate in the fun. She bounces on the bed wildly; her father lets her do it while keeping the baby safely out of her range.

Back to Babyhood

The logic seems clear: being a baby provokes great quantities of loving attention; acting just like this baby should bring the same love and attention.

Almost all children come to this conclusion after having watched their newborn sister or brother for a while. They take up some of their old ways in order to regain the feeling of being pampered.

Most parents recognize this regression for what it is, and don't become overly concerned. They will give in to the older child and allow him or her to have a bottle or a diaper for a while again. Once this desire is satisfied and more grownup things are offered, the phase passes. Sometimes extra attention from a grandparent, uncle, or teacher helps. The child returns to his or her more mature ways and goes about seeking attention and reward by age-appropriate behavior.

Since he has seen his new baby sister being fed, Morgan wants to be spoon-fed his breakfast. Other children may refuse to dress themselves or tie their shoelaces; and some "forget" their toilet training for a time after the baby's birth. In a few days Morgan felt satisfied and forgot about wanting to be fed.

With an ever-present cracker in his hand, Morgan spent a lot of his time under his new sister's bed for a few days. He called it his garage. We know of another four year old who called the underside of his baby sister's bed "his jail" once the bars were down.

Morgan also liked to try out the baby's crib. He laughed uproariously when he saw that he could touch both ends with his head and feet because he was so much bigger than the baby.

Regression and One Antidote

Especially when he is tired at the end of the day, Andrew seems to need his thumb and his favorite blanket since his little sister was born. Both his father and his mother understand this need to be small again; they know it will not last long. But they also encourage him to want to grow up, and be big and tall. They tell him how much he has grown recently, and Andrew beams happily.

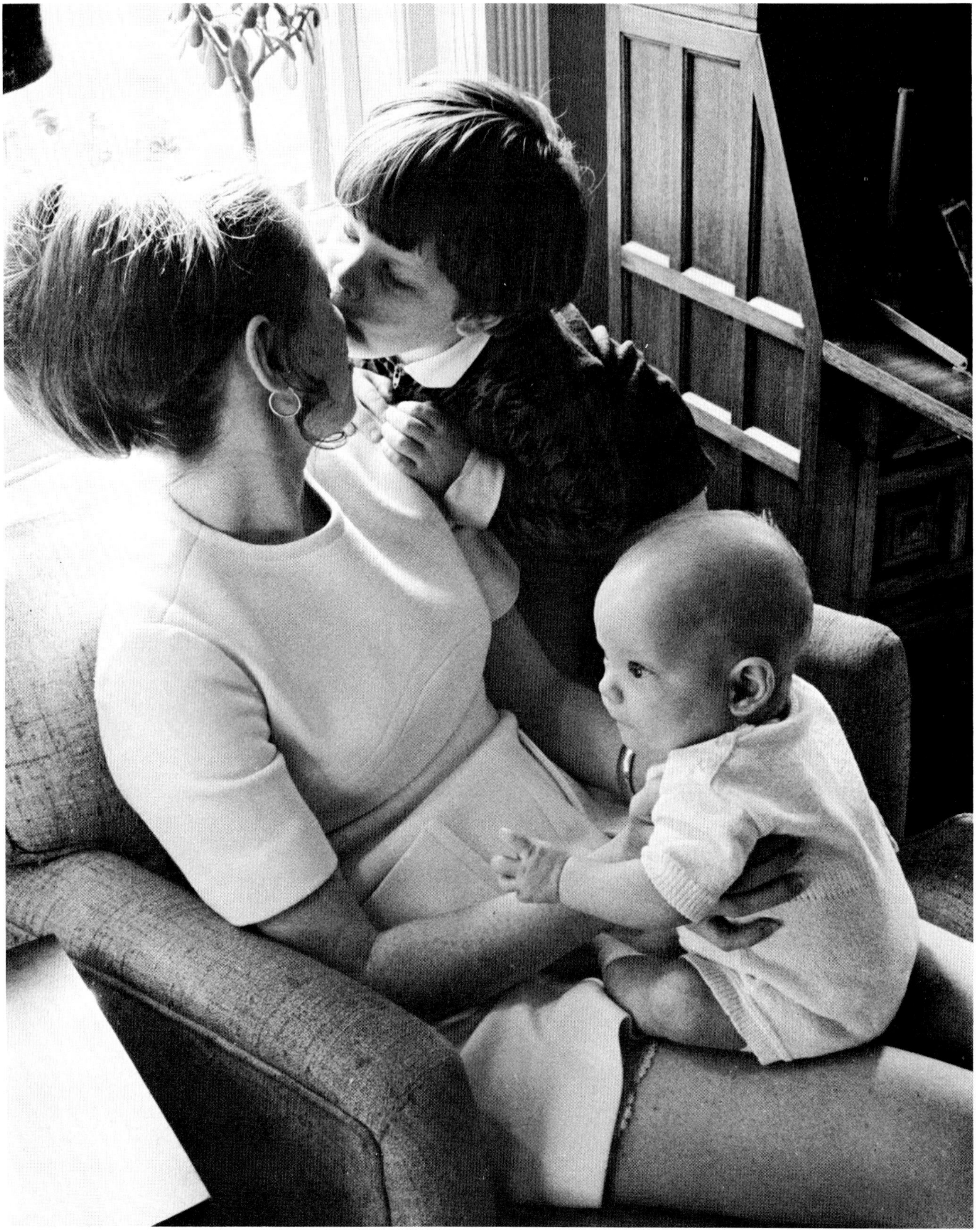

Special Time for Chris

It is easier said than done, but, evidently, giving some extra-special time to the older child without the presence of the new baby can work wonders in restoring his or her spirits. A baby takes lots of time to take care of, but it is worth going to some trouble to free enough time for the older one for a special story during the day or an excursion to the zoo. Here Chris gives his mother a big kiss when she says she will take him to the park and ride with him on the merry-go-round.

The Parson Family

Perhaps it isn't even fair to show the photographs of this family during the first days of little Caitlin's life: it all looks too too happy and easy. But yes, it *can* happen this way—especially when both parents work from their home and are around to satisfy their three little girls' needs. Maya, at eight, is the oldest; she has not had an easy time when her sister Fairley arrived two years ago. But now, she is all good will and helpfulness.

Maria Parson was able to give every one of her children plenty of love, supported by her husband's presence and by her mother's helpful weeklong visit from a far-away state.

Fairley is two years old, a sunny and sensitive child. But evidently there is plenty of speculation going on in her head at this moment as she sees her four-day-old baby sister in her mother's arms responding to her embrace.

Meeting the New Baby

Later in the day, she comes to see the baby. At first, she hesitates to approach her, but, with the encouragement of her mother, she gently touches the baby's hand. The baby gurgles, and Fairley smiles happily.

A New Addition to the Family

The first day at home with the baby is coming to an end, with father, mother, and their two older girls relaxing on the sofa. Grandma is holding the baby, which is not only a pleasure for her, but also gives the parents a chance to concentrate on their two older children.

Fairley and her father have a warm, close relationship which will not be changed by the arrival of another child.

A few weeks later, Fairley and Caitlin share their father's lap; Fairley is smiling even though the baby is pulling her hair.

Father Helps

Eight-year-old Maya is reading her father a story she wrote in school that day; Maria is changing the baby's diaper. Fairley is imitating her mother by undressing her own doll.

The family has absorbed the arrival of the new baby. It looks as if she had brought nothing but happiness to the Parsons.

The Smith Family

Here is another family with a new baby. After two girls, little Win has joined them. The two girls have different ways of adjusting to the newcomer.

Heather is nearly five. She looks proud and comfortable holding her baby brother. Having suffered from the usual jealousy when her sister was born, she is starting to feel the prestige of being the oldest.

Christina is nearly three and is used to being very close to her mother. Now she wants to be close both to her and the baby.

Helping to Feed the Baby

Her mother allows Christina to give Win his bottle; but as soon as he needs to be burped, she feels excluded. When Mother resumes the feeding, Christina kisses the baby's head. Her mother carefully watches to make sure her daughter is gentle enough not to hurt the delicate soft spot on the baby's head.

New Attachments

Heather is a sensitive child who is aware of the feelings and relationships of everyone around her. She still finds herself feeling left out once in a while, especially when the two younger ones play together.

FIGHTING

Adults are usually uncomfortable when they witness their children's acts of aggression and hostility, wishing the children's differences could be settled rationally and calmly.

What happens when children fight? What should parents do? Why do children fight so often? Can anything good come out of a fight? What are they really fighting about anyway?

Since fighting is so common among children, it must serve some universal purpose. It is less common among adults, so children must have learned to get along with others and solve their differences in ways that are acceptable in today's adult society.

Fighting seems to have both negative and positive sides. The negative aspects are obvious. But let's not overlook that the expression of angry feelings may be healthier than hiding or repressing them all the time.

There are several reasons why children fight. One of the most common centers around possessions. These fights can be based on real needs and desires for particular toys or objects; but they can also reflect other kinds of conflicts, such as assertion of power and control.

The second section of this chapter shows some of the physical fighting that parents find so hard to bear.

Another kind of fighting can be called roughhousing, a socially acceptable outlet for many aggressive feelings.

And finally, children often fight in order to attract their parents' attention. These fights usually erupt just when parents decide to spend some time on their own pursuits.

Fighting over Possessions

Children constantly fight over toys and other possessions. How many times do parents hear "It's *mine!*" "I had it first!" "He has *my* toy!" "She grabbed it!"

Sometimes children really want to play with a particular toy, work with a red piece of collage material, or wear nothing but one specific shirt. These are real, pragmatic reasons, and when they are challenged, a fight is liable to follow. At other times, children want something for its symbolic value. Little sister wants a pen simply because her brother has it. Or big brother asserts his power over little sister by taking her favorite toy.

Most toddlers go through a "possessive" stage. Everything and everyone is labeled by them as "*mine!*" Learning to share and to respect someone else's property are important tasks during the early childhood years.

Holidays are often prime time for fights between siblings. A great deal of excitement and anticipation accompanies birthdays, Christmas, and other holidays. It is hard for parents to satisfy each individual child and to succeed in preventing jealous counting and weighing of the presents.

Fighting over Possessions

Five-year-old Nina is crying. Her three-year-old sister has managed to take possession of the ring. Alexandra stands defiant and tenacious. Nina, though bigger and stronger, isn't trying to pull Alex off the ring. Her solution is to cry for help.

The moment Susan started to use the swing, her older sister Wendy felt that that's what she wanted to do, too. Since she is stronger, she wins; Susan will have to wait and rely on Mother to make sure that Wendy understands that might is not right.

That's Mine!

Four-year-old Tad has a big container of crayons. His eighteen-month-old sister wants them for herself. She is not satisfied with the two her brother has given her as a token. Tad doesn't seem upset here: Marguerite is obviously not going to get them. His expressions would have been quite different if his sister were pulling at the crayons container.

Now whose toy is it? Who had it first? The children are both angry and sure of their right of possession. Convincing these two to take turns and share the toy will not be easy. Maybe there is an attractive substitute around?

Quarreling over a Favorite Toy

Seven-year-old Billy has been playing with his favorite truck. All of a sudden, he feels his four-year-old brother Nat literally breathing down his neck in his desire to play with the beautiful toy.

In a generous moment, Billy has allowed Nat to have a turn; but now he cannot get the truck back from Nat. Father has come in, alerted by the loud argument. He tries to learn what the problem is from Billy.

Then he tells Nat that Nat has to return his brother's toy. Neither child wants to give in, so Father tries a new strategy. He suggests that Billy find Nat a substitute toy. There must be something that the little one would accept in trade.

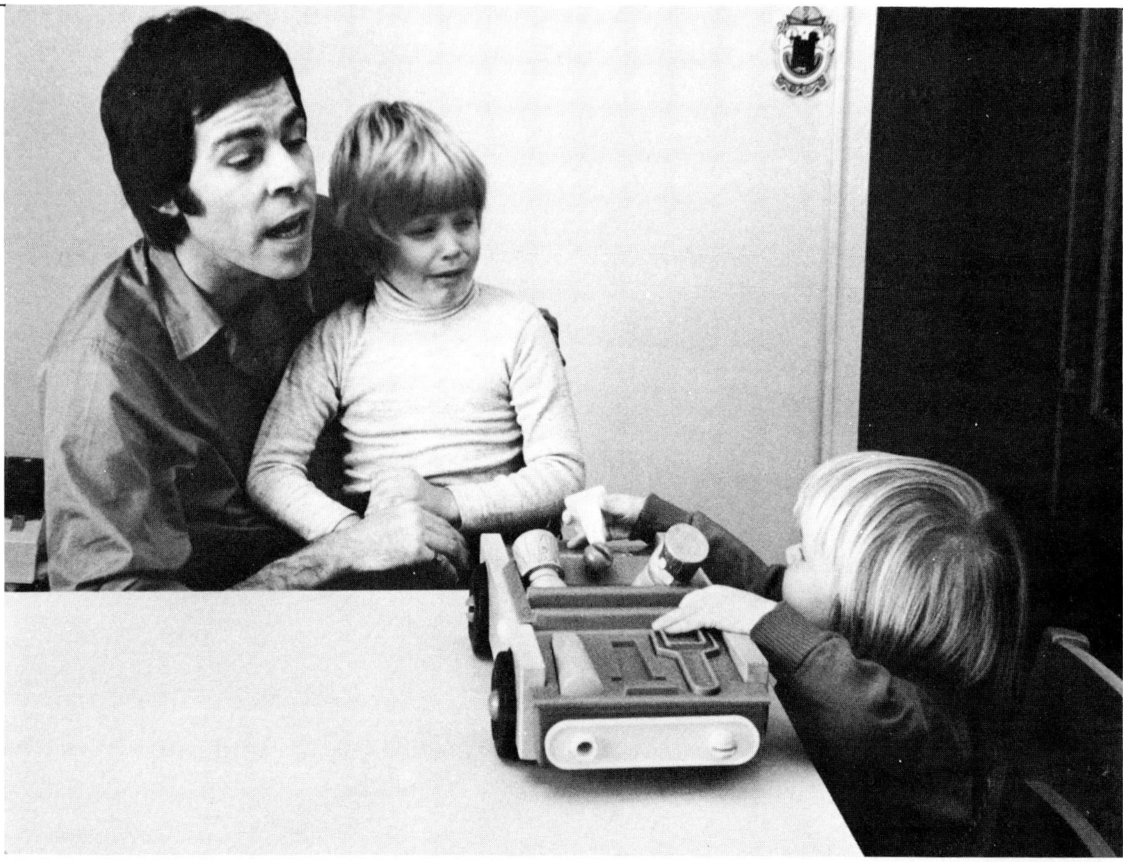

Reaching an Understanding

Billy chooses a small merry-go-round. He has seen Nat admire the toy, eager to make it work.

Nat accepts the trade but still has his eye on the truck.

All is well. Billy is back in sole possession of the truck, and Nat has just made the discovery of how to make the merry-go-round work by pushing it just so. He feels every bit as clever as Billy.

I am John; I am twenty-five years old now; these pictures bring back many mixed feelings. I was five years old then, and my little brother Gerry was three. It is hard to accept that we did all that yelling and crying over who would use the tricycle. It is true that I loved it and that I had a hard time giving Gerry a turn on it. I see that I did everything to block his path and even knock him off the tricycle with my head.

Looking Back on a Quarrel

A Row over a Tricycle

My mother picked up Gerry to tell him that he would get the tricycle from me when I outgrew it.

I notice that when I got my bike back I didn't pedal off at once; I had won the bicycle, but Mother was hugging Gerry.

Physical Fighting

For the most part, people who live in today's world believe that they should solve their problems by talking about them. They complain to someone when they believe they have been "wronged." If they don't succeed with a direct complaint, they appeal to some impartial authority to resolve the differences. People who do otherwise are often labeled as dangerous, violent, maladjusted, or even criminal.

It is amazing how these beliefs develop so universally, as children grow up to be members of civilized society. It seems like a long road to go from the loud screams of fury and flailing limbs of an angry infant to the rational discourse of two adults arguing their case before a judge. The road is made more difficult for most children since their parents give out several—often contradictory—messages.

When questioned, most parents will say that it is very important to teach children to fight with words instead of fists. "You tell her you don't like being pushed!" "Ask her why she is screaming at you!" "Tell her the toy is yours and you need it now." These are all stock phrases that children can use when another child hurts them or takes away something from them. "Tell me if she doesn't give your toy back to you." "Don't hit him, tell your father about it." "Find the teacher and tell her who hit you."

There is equally strong desire on the part of parents to see that their children not only learn to talk through their problems, but that they learn to defend themselves if it becomes necessary. "Don't fight" is said in virtually the same breath as "Well, kick him back if he doesn't stop kicking you" and "Take your toy back if she won't return it."

Siblings probably have more fights with each other than with other children. Some of this must be due to their constant contact; some of it to the special kind of teasing, jealousy, and ambivalence they feel.

While physical fighting and even heated verbal battles are upsetting to the children doing the fighting, it is equally upsetting to other children watching the fighting. Sometimes another sibling will join in a fight, even if it has nothing to do with him or her; sometimes the third child will run for a parent or babysitter to come and stop the fighting. At other times the noncombatant will feel so left out of all the fuss that he or she will do something drastic to draw attention away from the fighters.

It is important not to overlook the chance for growth that can occur when siblings fight, even when a few punches are thrown and a few kicks felt. Children learn to deal with their anger by ventilating it in fights with someone close. Rarely do these fights have permanent effects. More than likely, the fighters make up and return to being friends. Thus children experience the flare-ups of angry feelings, the attempts to express them, others' reaction to the anger, and a resolution of the relationship following the disappearance of the anger.

Darcy is about to hit her older brother with a box because she is so angry about having been left out of a game that Quentin has started with her baby sister. But however strong her frustration, at the last moment the blow is deflected from Quentin's head and she hits the toys instead.

Wails of yelling and crying from the front yard. Mother, who was busy in the house, opens the door to find out what is happening. She sees her ten-year-old son Chris standing defiantly over his younger brother Andrew. In between sobs, Andrew tells her that Chris has just hit him. Chris screams that Andrew has taken his bike without his permission and has just damaged it.

Mother has no way of knowing precisely what has happened here. She is, nonetheless, being asked to render a court decision with fairness and justice. In frustration, she might simply say: "I don't care what happened. Both of you stop yelling and make up!" Sometimes, when both children seem to be at fault to some degree, it is necessary to separate them and deal with sorting out the facts later, after everyone has had time to cool off.

Anger Breaks Out

Ten-year-old Judy is trying to force the knife from her brother Tom's hand since he has been using it to "draw" on the placemats with it. When her mother had to leave for the day, she had asked Judy to be "in charge." But Tom does not like to be bossed around by his sister and is waiting for their father to render justice.

Giving one sibling power over the other for any extended period of time can be dangerous. The one in charge may have trouble knowing the limits of her power or giving it up. Short periods of responsibility can bring some siblings close together, but prolonged "pseudo responsibility" can lead to resentment and conflicts over actual and imagined role relations.

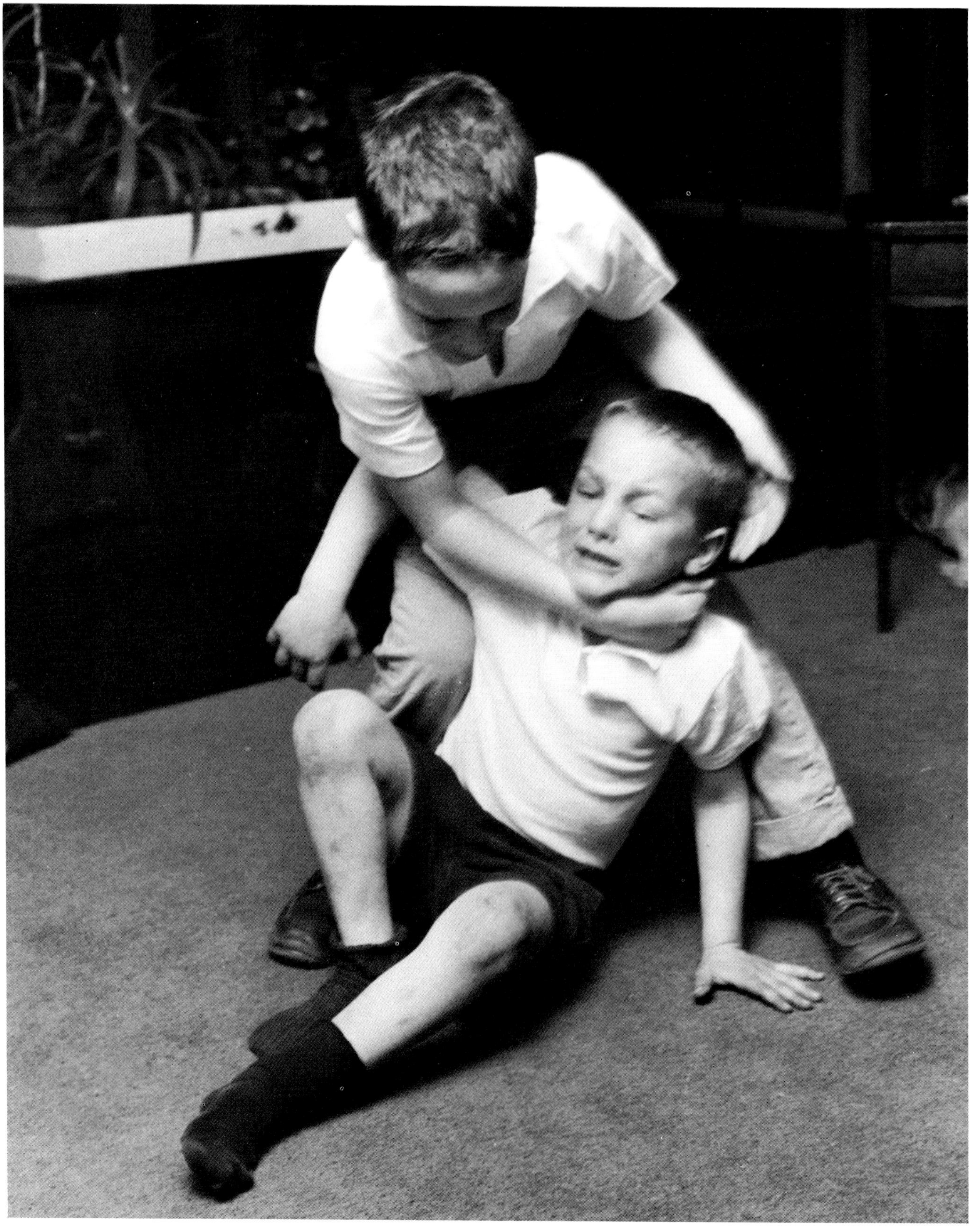

The Battle Rages

In a family with four boys very close in age, there is bound to be a lot of physical fighting since each one is trying to assert his will over the next younger.

Roughhousing

Roughhousing serves many functions. For some children, playing at fighting is a socially acceptable way to express aggression. For others, roughhousing allows them the physical intimacy they reject under other circumstances. After they feel "grown up," boys are especially likely to avoid cuddling and hugging; yet they crave intense roughhousing with their fathers and mothers.

During these encounters, children usually believe that the grownup will not hurt them or allow things to get out of hand. So they can reverse the power position and assert temporary authority over the adult.

When sisters and brothers try to roughhouse with a parent at the same time, the situation becomes even more complicated. They seem to enjoy the cooperation of ganging up on one of the parents, but at the same time they compete to outshine each other in fighting skill. It takes an energetic, ingenious parent to keep things at a reasonable level of excitement while fighting with several children without anyone getting hurt.

John and Paul often roughhouse. Their little sister Julia, six, has decided to take part in the fun. But the vehemence of the tussle frightens her and, as she nearly disappears under the weight of her two brothers, she starts crying. The boys comfort her. But that smile on their faces seems to express more than concern and love—it also shows a little bit of victory of two strong "men" who can take what this little girl cannot.

Rough and Tumble

Brooke usually doesn't like to fight or play as rough as her brother Sean. But in the pillow fight she holds her own. The safety of the soft pillow allows her to fight on equal terms. Pillow fights are a good substitute for real hitting.

Andrew's expression tells us a lot: Do the grownups approve of his roughhousing with his little sister Abigail, one, even though he is now treating her pretty rough? Will Abigail continue to enjoy this play or revolt against the weight of her brother on top of her? It is really amazing how patient most second children can be when it comes to putting up with the rigors of their older siblings' attention.

Two-year-old Susan likes to entice her older brother Steven into games that often end by his being blamed for becoming too rough. Most parents know that it is usually impossible to tell who started what and why. The important thing is to have both children stop once the game becomes too violent.

Roughhousing with Parents

Billy, eight, and Nathaniel, five, have a young, energetic father who loves to play with them; they often roughhouse together. He knows just how far he can allow the children to go, how to defend himself, and how to stop the two boys from continuing the fight once he withdraws.

Observers often comment that parents roughhouse more vigorously with their sons than with their daughters. Some attribute this to a cultural bias in which boys are expected to be rougher and less fearful of fighting than girls. It is hard to determine how much the parents' expectations reinforce an inborn disposition. In any case, these days young parents make sure that they give their daughters plenty of strong physical exercise and ball-play. Here we see Chrissy being swung vigorously by her mother.

Fighting for Parental Attention

Children seem to believe that parents exist solely in order to satisfy their needs. This is not surprising since most of their interaction with parents center around being fed, bathed, clothed, and entertained. It is difficult for children to understand that parents have their own relationships and needs.

When parents talk on the phone, for example, children invariably become upset. The baby usually starts to cry just when mother is picking up the phone to call a friend; the six year old discovers he needs help with his homework just as his parents want to sit down to plan their vacation.

Fighting between children often breaks out when parents have sent them off to play by themselves. To gain control over a parent's attention, a child may provoke his or her sibling into fighting, especially when direct attempts to gain attention have failed. Awareness of this tendency may help parents deal with the fights that break out when they try to exclude the children from a discussion or activity.

Children often ask for the impossible: equal room with their brother or sister on a parent's lap; equal time of care giving when the other sibling is ill or younger or in special need of comforting. If they think that a sibling is getting too much attention, they will pick a fight simply to draw attention to themselves. These fights should be treated differently from fights due to other, more realistic causes.

Father and mother are trying to read the Sunday papers. Their two daughters, six and eight, know their parents like to do so in peace. But no sooner do the children start to play outside than they get into an argument and run back in to have the parents settle it. In this case, the children were able to leave the parents out of their arguments.

Mother is trying to conduct an important conversation on the phone. Her children, Chris, five, and Jonathan, two, would like her to pay attention to them instead. They start to tussle playfully at first, pulling the bed sheet, throwing the pillow, making noise. When this does not get Mother's attention, Jonathan starts crying in frustration.

What Can a Mother Do?

Mother wants peace and a cup of coffee. Instead, all hell breaks loose among her three children, so they can get her attention back. Her solution is to pick up the baby, try to ignore the two older ones—and finish her coffee.

Mother is trying to cook dinner. This is now the third time she has been interrupted to stop her children from fighting. Both her words and her body language finally get through to her children; they feel she really means it when she says: "I cannot take one more minute of this fighting!"

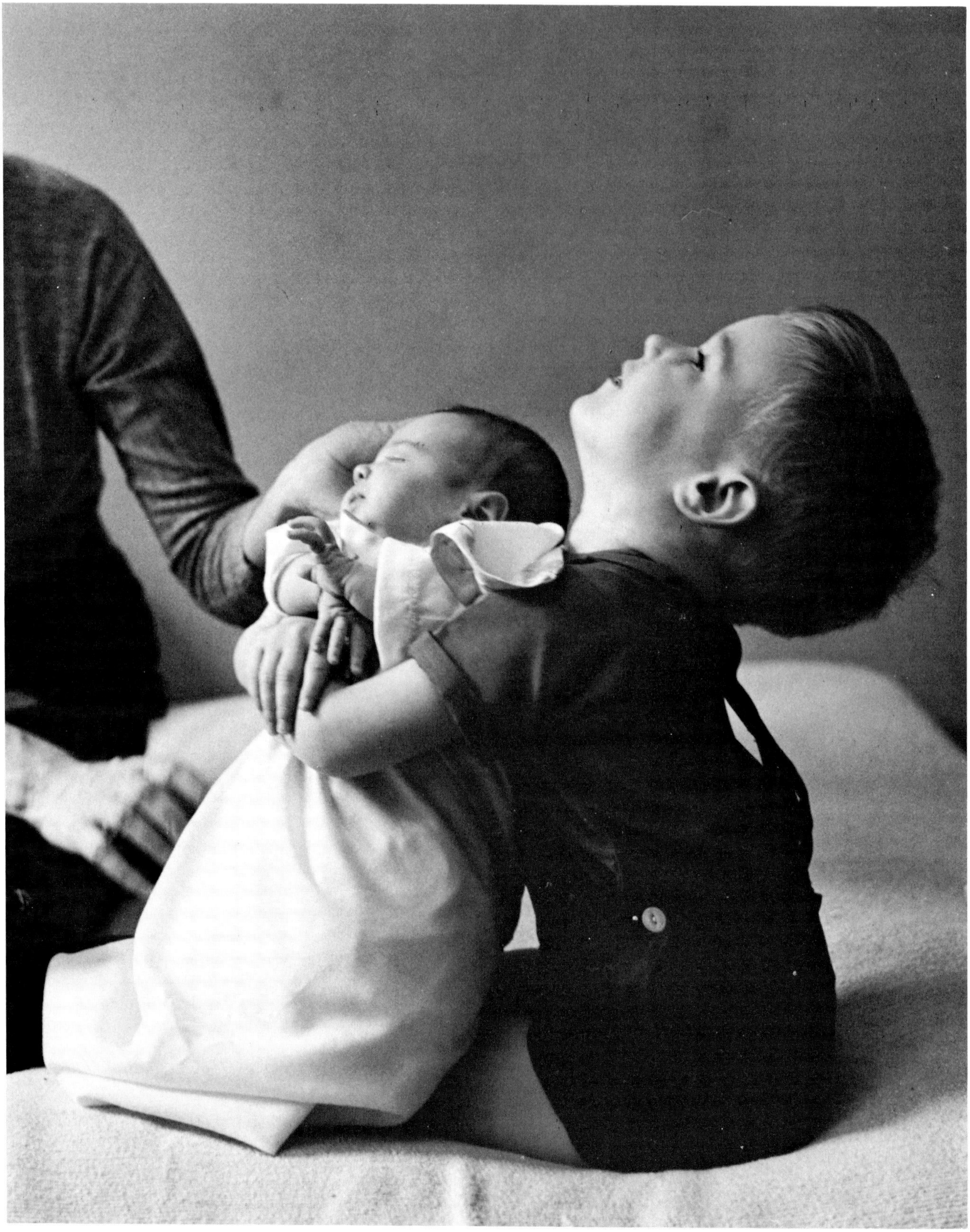

LOVING

As children grow up, they need to learn to get along with people. Their first intimate relationships are formed within the family. These influence the friendships they form as they mature. Siblings offer each other a sustained close relationship during which each will experience the exhilaration of love and the desperation of rejection.

Despite temperamental differences and jealousies, brothers and sisters are stuck with each other; they cannot divorce each other when things go bad. They have to work out a way of living together. This will help them to get along with others and form positive intimate relationships in adulthood.

Their common experiences bind sisters and brothers. Even fighting can be healthy and promote closeness if siblings vent their feelings. But fighting also has to be kept under control to minimize the negative side of the ambivalence that characterizes almost all sibling relationships.

How does the positive side develop? Children watch and touch each other; a baby often responds happily to an older brother's or sister's cuddling or tickling; older siblings find pleasure in playing together. One can often catch them looking at each other in wonderment or show in beautiful, nonverbal ways how happy they are with each other.

It would be hard to overemphasize the role that the parents' love plays in deciding whether their children will love each other or even learn to love anyone. One has to receive love in order to be able to give it.

Love is tenderness, caring, consideration, and a willingness to communicate. But it is also justice; the creation of an atmosphere in which each child gets a fair hearing and consistent punishments and rewards.

There is no way that parents can love their children equally; each relationship will be different. This does not matter as long as love governs them all.

Leaning away from another person usually expresses negative feelings. But in this case, three-year-old Johnny seems to lean back as if suddenly overwhelmed by the love he feels for his lovely new baby sister Debbie.

Babies Are Lovable

Eric, four, is smiling as he looks down on his little sister Neisha. But this smile says more: it speaks of tenderness, curiosity, love.

It is fortunate that a baby is so very appealing and can call forth such loving smiles from older brothers and sisters. This helps balance the negative feelings that are nearly universal when children must share their parents with a newcomer.

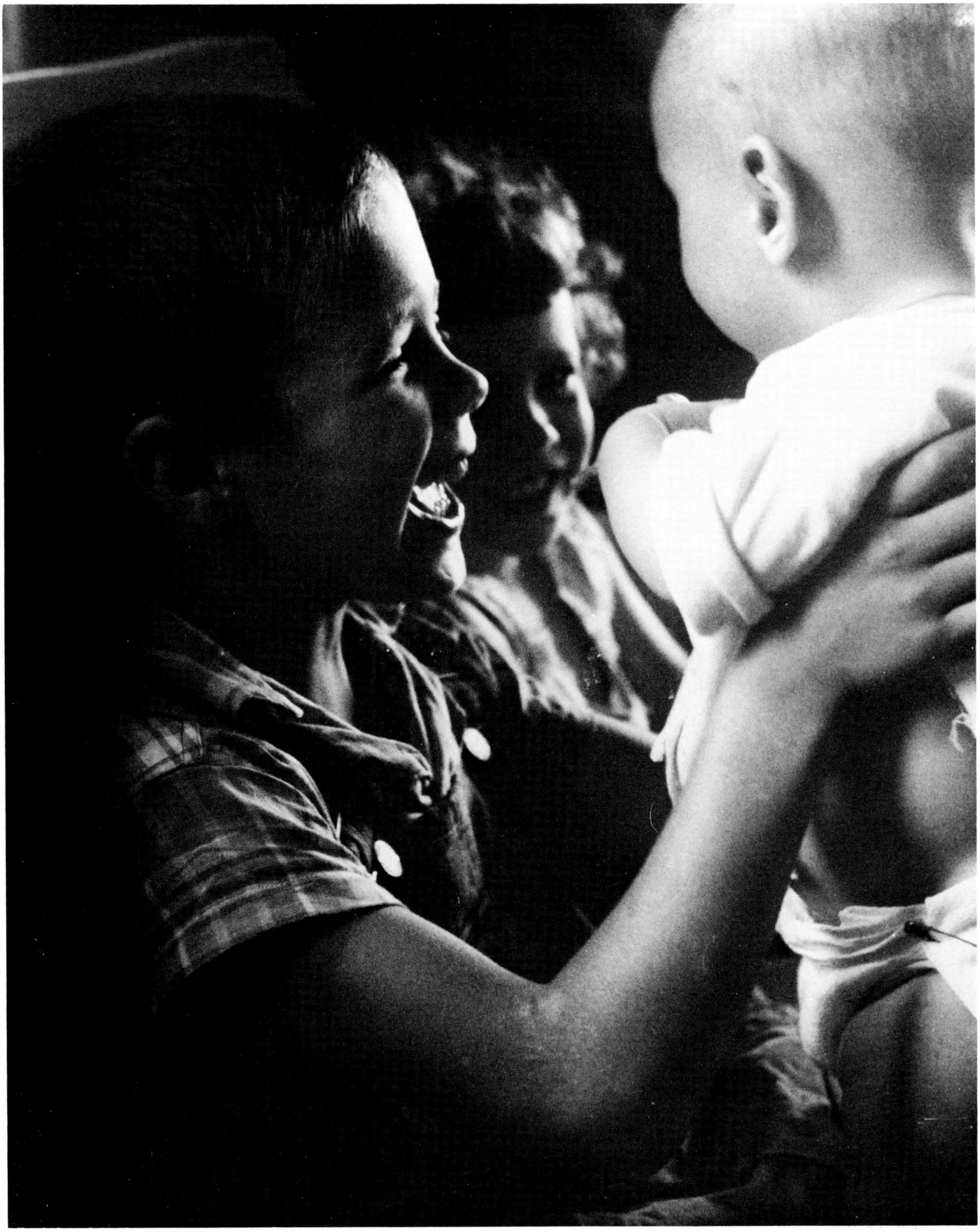

Expressions of Love

Trouble seems to be brewing when one-year-old Pegge notices that her sister Chrissy has taken possession of *her* chair. But she cannot resist Chrissy's provocative smile and her invitation to come and give her a hug. So love has triumphed, even though that most common of war cries—"*Mine!*"—has been involved.

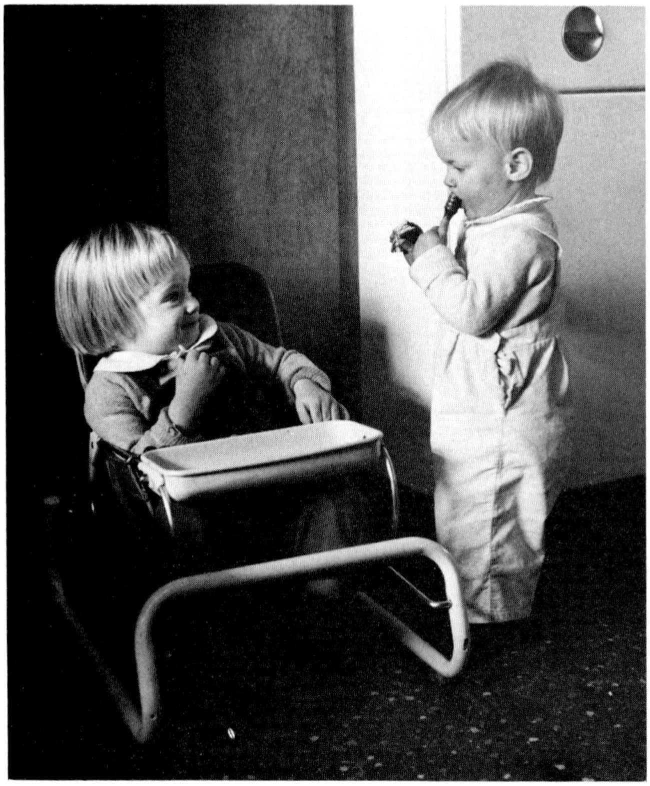

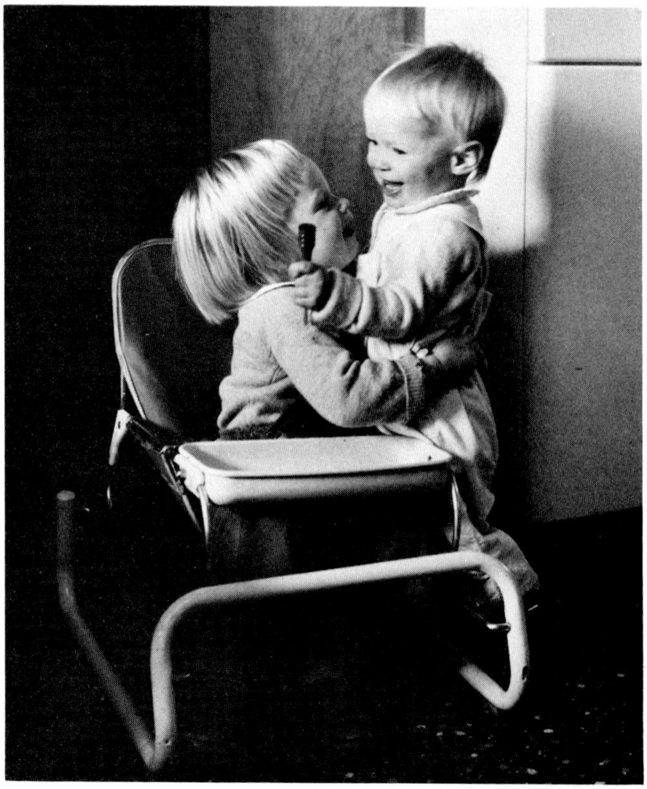

Six-year-old David and nine-month-old Laurie come from a large family whose members express their love and affection in many nonverbal ways.

Comforting

One of the nicest ways that sisters and brothers express their love is by comforting each other in times of distress. Sometimes, when they are unhappy, another child, who is close in age, can understand better than an adult, especially when the pain is of a psychological rather than physical nature. The six year old is probably in a better position to understand the hurt of his four-year-old sister, who is desolate because her best friend would not sit next to her at nursery school, than a parent, who has already forgotten how much such an incident can hurt.

When parents are the source of distress, the comfort that siblings give each other is especially important. Everyone has heard complaints like "Mommy is mean; she won't let me have my candy" told to a sibling in the hope of comfort.

When there is tension between parents, or when external life pressures such as a serious illness, death, unemployment, or divorce impose stress on the family, the love that sisters and brothers feel for each other brings them together for mutual support and comfort. It is amazing how unerringly even small children pick up the emotional currents in a family; it is good to know that they gain strength from comforting each other.

Five-year-old Nanna has been playing "little mother" to her brother Sam ever since he was born. When their parents got a divorce, she felt he needed her more than ever. It is a heavy responsibility for someone so young; but her situation was made easier by the love and caring of her three older siblings.

Helping Hands

One-year-old Pegge looks a bit surprised at the way her brother Howard, four, has chosen to cheer her up. But his energetic intervention does make her forget that mother had just taken away a pair of scissors from her, saying that she couldn't play with them.

Seven-year-old Laura is quick to help and comfort her little sister Claire who had taken a spill during roller-skating. She feels responsible, as she was the one from whom Claire learned to skate.

Consoling

Jeremy, 9, and Justin, 7, are spending a lot of time together in a place where their mother is working. There are few if any other children around, and the people at this summer camp treat them like grownups. They behave accordingly in a grown fashion, with much less squabbling and childish scrapping than usually. They have also become very close without their usual friends of their own age. When Jeremy is in a bad mood, Justin finds ways to make him smile.

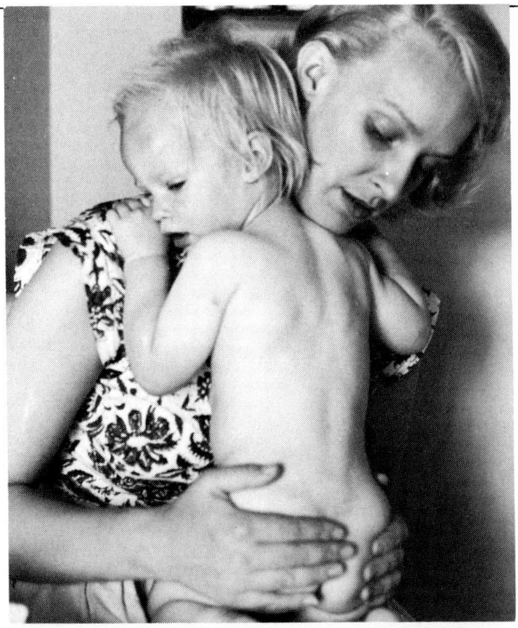

Children learn from their parents. If their need to be comforted is met by the adults around them, they will be able to comfort others.

Whenever Chrissy feels upset, her mother comforts her. Mother does this in a way that does not deny that sadness and anger are a part of life: she just tells Chrissy that it is all right to feel this way, but that there are many reasons why she will feel better soon.

When Chrissy hears her baby sister cry, she runs to her to comfort her.

One of those "watershed points" in physical development between siblings is the time when a four year old is ready for his first tricycle while the two-year-old sister can only admire it.

Play

One of the nicest things about having a brother or a sister is that you always have someone to play with. Play creates a strong bond between children. A three year old, who is struggling with accepting a new baby, will get his payoff when he will have someone to play house with—even if it is too early on a Sunday morning to ask a friend over.

When children engage in make-believe games, they tend to act out many of their unexpressed feelings and desires. For example, in her wish to exert authority over an older brother, a little girl may insist that he play the role of "baby" or "patient."

There is a three-year difference between Bonnie and Todd. One of their favorite games is playing house in a plywood tree house built by their father.

Half of pretend house or doctor play is usually taken up with deciding on their different roles.

Having Fun Together

Nothing is sweeter than forbidden fruit. Cathy, four, is taking advantage of her mother's absence to bounce on the bed; her baby sister is enjoying the feeling, too.

Sexual Feelings

Sexual curiosity is an important part of physical contact among siblings. Most young children are curious to see if other children have the same parts as they do or if they are different. The touching and caressing among young siblings usually transcends the traditional ideas about sex in physical contact.

Accepting sensuality as part of intimacy is an important lesson; learning to pull away from that intimacy when it goes beyond the limits of simple tenderness is also an important lesson of growing up and usually learned in the sister-brother relationship.

Many adults prefer to ignore the kind of early sex play that brothers and sisters engage in They can also become so upset that they overreact and punish the children for doing something that the children cannot understand as being wrong.

The mother of this brother and sister, aged four and two, handles things differently. She believes that free expression of sensual feelings will serve her children well in helping them to grow up as uninhibited adults who accept their own sexuality.

Play Can Mean Different Things at Different Ages

For a while now, the two-year age difference between Nina and Alexandra seemed like a few months instead of two years. But then, Nina became interested in boys and—until Alexandra catches up—she is one step further ahead on the development to a full-fledged teenager.

Parents who genuinely enjoy playing with their children can find many games and hobbies to share with them. Nothing will kindle the children's enthusiasm more than a parent who genuinely loves an activity like painting or swimming.

Teaching

In many large families, children are expected to teach their brothers and sisters many small tasks. Both teacher and pupil are rewarded in this exchange, which also results in added independence. The mutual cooperation that comes with teaching and learning helps build the sibling relationship and enhances the children's mutual respect for each other.

Good teachers are able to break down a complex task into small "do-able" parts. Tying a shoelace, for instance, has become an unconscious movement to a grownup; but a child who has just recently learned to do it is acutely aware of what is involved and will be able to teach a younger sibling much better.

Here, three-year-old Todd watches as his sister Bonnie, six, shows him how to tie his shoelaces.

Six-year-old Nanna is teaching her little brother Sam the intricacies of a small pinball game. He soon catches her enthusiasm and starts to enjoy the game, too.

Learning by Imitation

Seven-year-old, left-handed Laura is doodling in a copybook; her three-year-old sister Claire is watching her intently. When Laura notices that Claire is really trying to learn from her, she changes the pen from left hand to the right, so that Claire, who is right-handed, can identify the movements better. She also helps her trace some lines, and soon—success! Claire is able to draw the beginnings of a pussycat.

Teaching Sports

Julia, five, just got her first real bicycle; her brother Paul, nine, is helping her learn. She is a bit scared, but she trusts him to hold on to the bike if she should lose her balance.

Laura and Claire again, this time at the playground. Laura is teaching her younger sister roller skating. She is more than teaching: she is there to lean on, to encourage, to cheer. No wonder Claire is learning faster than she would from any adult.

GORDON

Teaching by Doing

When seven-and-a-half-year-old Justin saw that his nine-year-old brother was interested in chess, he took out a book from a library to learn the game and to try to beat him. In these pictures Justin's face lights up as he thinks he has outfoxed his brother; but in the next move he finds that his brother is going to win after all.

Fifteen-year-old Jane is a good cook. Her little sister Rhoda loves to help. Jane has found a way to teach her tasks like stirring the batter which will not ruin the cake and still satisfy Rhoda's desire to participate.

Learning from Parents

While she is making cookies herself, this mother has prepared some dough, a separate cookie sheet, and some simple instruments so that her two daughters, five-year-old Catherine and three-year-old Elizabeth, can make their own. She then lets them make cookies the way they wish and allows the older girl to teach the younger one.

The presence of a patient and interested parent can have a beneficial effect on the children's play, if that parent can control that urge to take over. Here, the father is holding the jack-in-the-box but lets his daughter Claire help her little brother Peter.

It isn't necessary to urge four-year-old Matthew to be patient when his two-year-old sister is still eating her breakfast, thus postponing the moment when they can all go out and play. His father's loving, patient mood is making Matthew feel the same way.

A Family Outing

During an autumn walk at the beach, this family made sand castles, ran at the edge of the water, and exchanged enthusiastic hugs in between. This is bound to make Billy and Nat feel that physical expression of feelings is wonderful. Back home, their father's clowning rendition of a favorite story makes them all laugh.

SPECIAL SITUATIONS

The first three chapters of this book deal with situations and issues that are common to all children: reactions to a new baby, fighting, loving. This chapter shows special situations and discusses issues that are unique to particular children: only children, middle children, half-brothers and half-sisters, adopted children, and twins.

The Only Child

Being an only child can have many rewards. One does not have to share the emotional and material resources of a family with another sibling; parents can spend more time with an only child than when many children claim their attention.

But there are some disadvantages, too. It can be lonely without another child for companionship, especially when the parents are busy. There could also be a great deal of pressure from the parents to satisfy their need to feel proud of their child and to be loved by him or her. An only child also misses out on the intimacy of living with a sibling.

The only child has much in common with the first-born—who was an only child for a while. The research literature shows that both tend to be achievers and "good" boys and girls. They are very conscious of rules; they are ready to take on responsibilities and strive hard to please the adults around them. They like the company of grownups and seek their support in times of stress.

Never having experienced the changes that the arrival of a new baby brings, only children are different in that they keep their place in the family. They may grow up to feel that life will fulfill all their expectations and that other people will be as giving as their parents were. Some only children find that they need help to make the transition from their long-standing role as "darling of the family" to responsible adult who can relate on equal terms in close personal relationships.

Henrik Learns Early

Seven-year-old Henrik is an only child. It is, of course, impossible to know whether he would have changed or stayed the same if he had had siblings. But it is hard not to think of him as an only child. He is independent, inventive in play, and happy in the company of his parents. They share most of their ideas and hobbies with him. He accompanies them on their trips. He is allowed to stay up for parties, where his general knowledge and self-assurance surprise many adults.

Naturally, some children his age seem pale and even boring compared to the adults; but as an only child, they are especially important to him.

Only Children

Emily is four years old. Being an only child, she has had less contact with other children. So every time her mother introduces her to new playmates, she prefers to sit on her mother's knee before venturing forth to play for a while.

But pretty soon she rejoins her mother, who is talking to her friends, and quietly sits there, listening to them. Emily is starting school in a few months, where she is sure to find children who interest her.

There is a look of sophistication on the face of Suzanne that belies her six years. In her short life she has gone through many difficulties.

The Middle Child

In a family with three children, the middle child is often thought to be at a disadvantage. The first-borns receive special attention not only because they were first, but because their birth was a completely new, magical experience for their parents. The third child is the baby of the family who needs special protection and leniency. But the middle child, being neither the first to accomplish something nor the most vulnerable because he or she is the smallest, has to fight for his or her special place.

If the first-born is much older than the middle child, both children can react as if they were first-borns. If the middle child is the only girl between two brothers, she is guaranteed a special place in the family. Others win their unique place by a combination of their personality and their roles. They are often the peacemakers of the family. They try hard to please adults and to be rewarded.

Darcy is three years old. She has an older brother and a baby sister. At times, Quentin's competent self-assurance and baby Jocelyn's cuteness seem to make her wonder about her own place in the family.

She often seems lost in her own world. Her body language expresses her serious attempt at solving some problems: her eyebrows are puckered, her hand is supporting her head.

Samantha Seeks Affection

It is hard to figure out who is the middle child in this closely spaced trio of sisters. They are close in every way, not only in age: they play together; they argue and laugh and share secrets together.

But, according to their mother, it is nearly always Samantha, the middle child, who comes to her or to her father for a quick, reassuring hug or kiss.

Stepsiblings

When parents remarry, their children must adjust to new mothers and fathers and to their new stepbrothers and stepsisters. If the new couple then has children of their own, the situation becomes even more complex. There may be a large age difference between the two or three sets of children; they must learn to get along without earlier experiences together. Their jealousy of each other's place in these complicated families can be intense.

When an only child finds himself with an instant set of sisters and brothers, he can feel particularly threatened. The hoped-for closeness may take a long time to develop. It is hard to see one's parent turn his or her attention not only to a new mate but also toward the children that are now part of the family. Beside love and patience, flexibility and a good sense of humor are needed to make a success of creating these new family units.

With his blend of charm and mischievousness, five-year-old Chris is once again holding the undivided attention of his family: his father and mother, his ten-year-old sister and his two stepbrothers, fifteen and seventeen, who spend weekends with them.

Adopted Children

Adopted children generally tend to react to their siblings in much the same way as nonadopted children. Since there seems to be more of a voluntary nature to the parents' "picking" a new sibling, adopted children may feel more anger and fear of being discarded than children who are not adopted.

In families where the adoption of children is followed by the birth of the parents' children, the situation can become even more complicated, especially when the children come from different cultures.

Whatever special problems come up with adopted children, none seems evident now with three-and-one-half-year-old Victoria and one-year-old Michael. Both came from Korea and were adopted when they were a few months old.

Twins

Whether identical or fraternal, twins share the same environment from the time they are conceived. Thus they have an unusually close emotional attachment to each other. They often develop a special language that no one else can understand or intrude upon. Content with each others' company, twins usually suffer less from the fear of separation that plague most young children when parents leave them with babysitters or when they have to go to school.

Twins, especially identical twins, may have difficulty seeing themselves as distinct from each other.

Raising twins can be difficult, especially when there are other children demanding attention. There can be a great temptation to deal with the twins as if they were a single unit. As small babies, they are fed and bathed together, and pushed to have the same sleeping schedule. While few parents still dress their twins in identical clothes, it simplifies their work to deal with them in identical ways. Sometimes this is just what is needed. But parents must be sensitive and recognize when the twins need to be treated differently in order to have a chance for individual development.

Nine-month-old identical twins Tatjana and Marina are amusing themselves with pulling a rag doll back and forth while waiting for lunch.

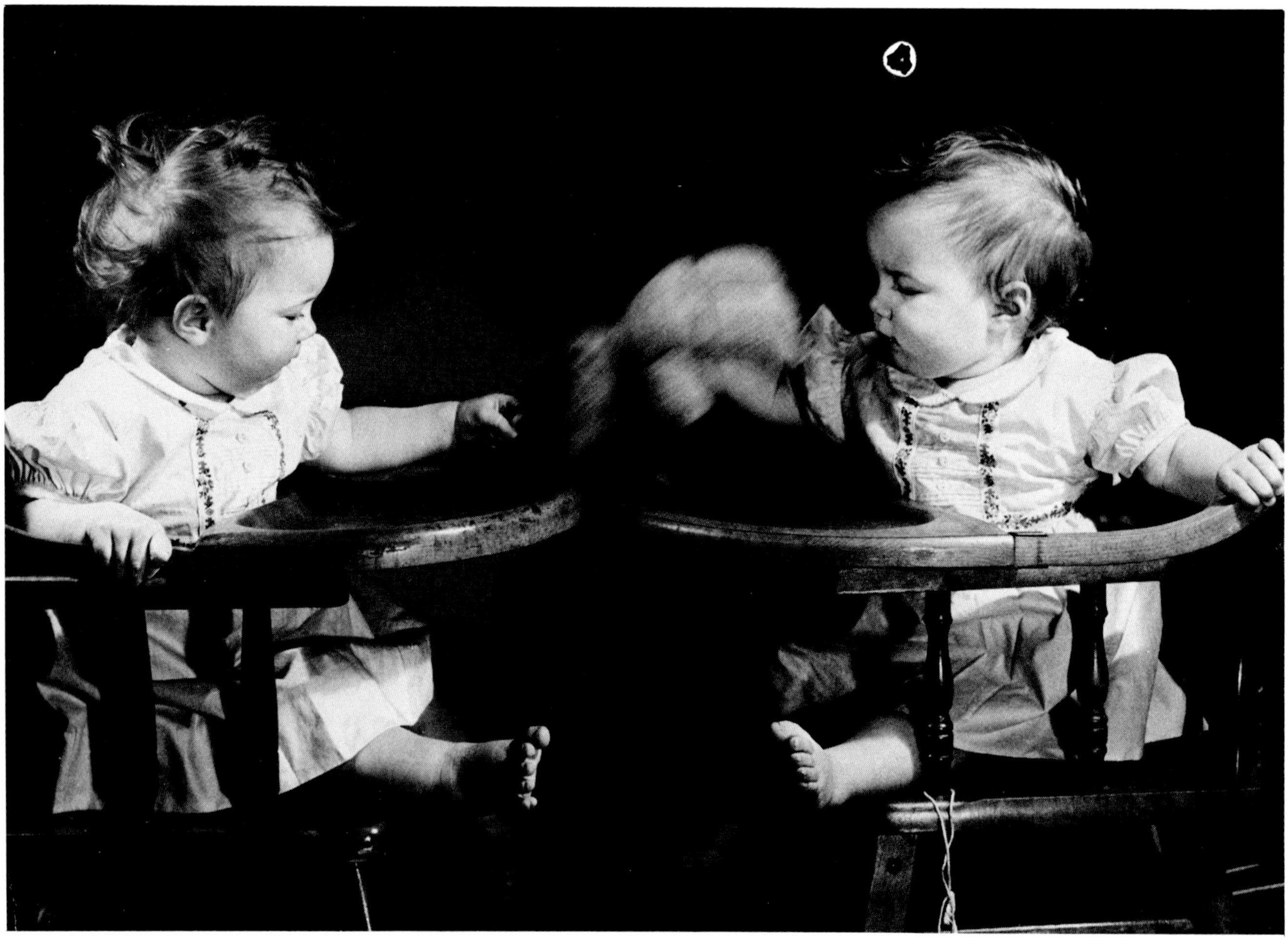

At age four, they are still inseparable and companionable.

Coping with Twins

A father's involvement in helping with the care of his children is never more crucial than in the case of twins. Just carrying two small babies is no easy task for a young mother. They seem to be getting hungry at the same time, too; so an extra hand is most welcome. Here Andrew and Jonathan are four months old; they are fraternal twins, but they look a lot alike.

While five-year-old fraternal twins Brooke and Sean are close friends and playmates, they are very different in temperament and personality. They also show their gender difference clearly. Brooke loves dolls; Sean is full of restless energy. Their parents have been careful to allow them to develop in accordance with their separate needs and interests.

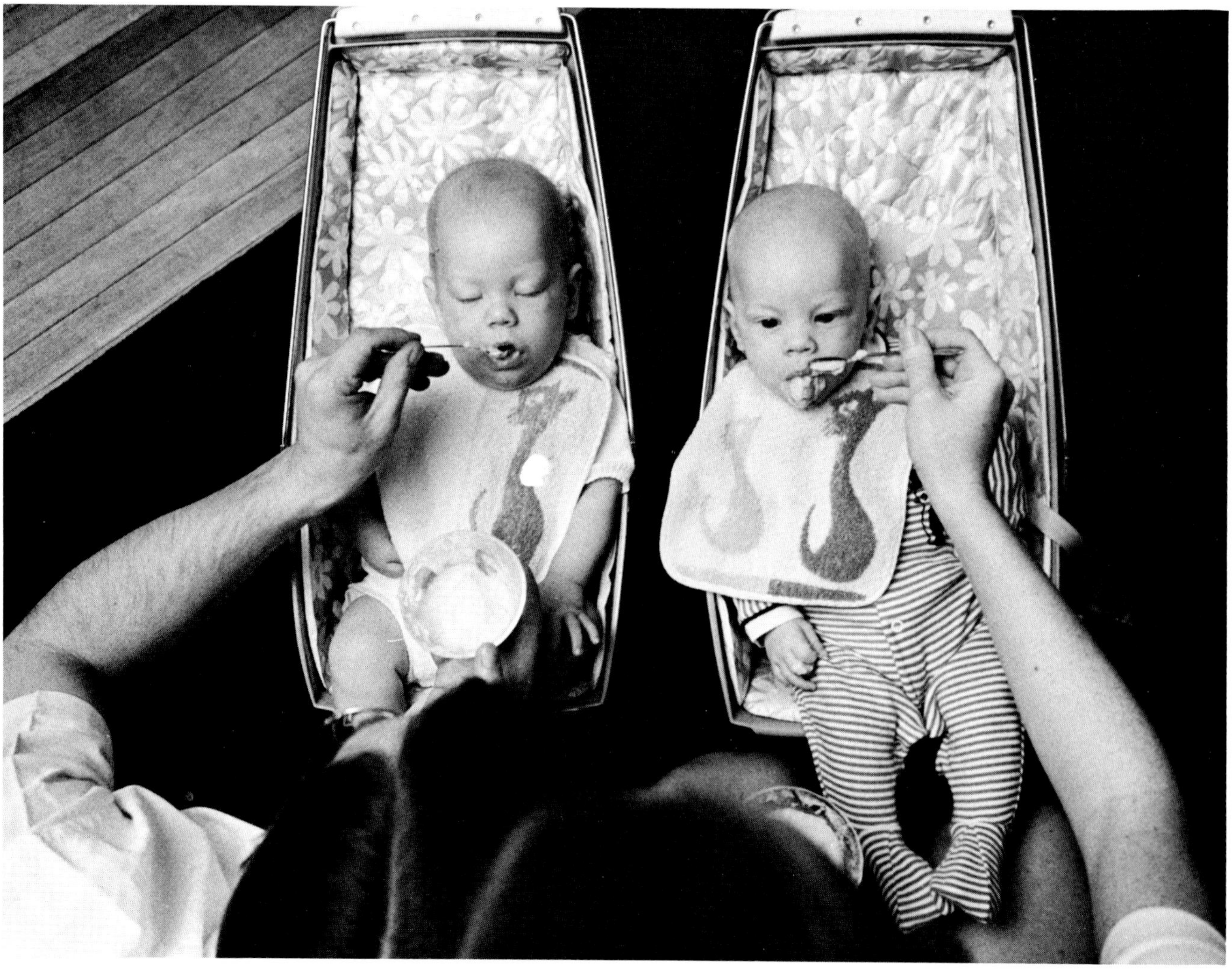

Fraternal Twins

Five-year-old fraternal twins Deborah and Jillian are growing at different rates. Pretty soon they won't even look like twins any more. This is all right with both of them and with their parents, who have always encouraged them to feel and act like two separate beings.

Preston and Kenton are four and a half years old; they really like to do the same things. This leads to some frustration for both of them since their abilities and rate of growth are far from identical. If one is better at a sport, the other practices harder in order to keep up with him.

1 Year Apart

THE EFFECT OF AGE DIFFERENCES

What is the ideal spacing of children in a family? How old should they be before they are able to adjust to the next child? What happens when children are spaced very closely or very far apart?

Obviously, there are no simple answers, no "correct" solutions that can apply to every family. Each first-born is different; children of the same age differ in their emotional maturity and in the rate at which they develop.

Psychologists offer some advice on family planning; they try to steer parents toward waiting at least three years between children. By that time, most children are secure in their relationship with their parents and have been able to separate from them. This means that they think of themselves as whole human beings and can function with some independence.

Children who are very close in age usually vie for parental attention and for the favored position in the family; they are competitive and resentful of each other's achievements. The famous James brothers, William and Henry, who were only fifteen months apart in age, carried on a lifelong, highly competitive relationship that affected their lives in every way.

There are, however, some advantages to having children close in age. The children tend to share many interests. This provides lasting bonds that can carry through into adult life.

Parents who delayed having children until they were in their thirties usually find that having them closely spaced is the only practical solution.

Like twins, very closely spaced children may have trouble finding their sense of separate identity. Like twins, they must learn to separate not only from their parents, but also from the sister or brother with whom they have developed an intense attachment.

On the other extreme are families where many years separate the birth of the children. Sometimes this is an unplanned occurrence; at other times parents decide to have more babies after their older children have grown up. In a time when divorce and remarriage are common occurrences, children may have to get used to large age differences between them and half brothers and sisters.

The photographs show children spaced as close as thirteen months and as far apart as thirteen years.

It would be fascinating to know what thirteen-month-old Julia has understood of the arrival of her tiny baby sister Olivia. Most of the time, she smiles glowingly, kissing and hugging her sister with all her might. It is only natural that she cannot comprehend that these hugs could hurt the baby. Luckily, her most patient and loving parents protect the baby without getting upset with Julia.

2 Years Apart

Chrissy is two years old in this photograph. Who knows what she has or has not understood about the arrival of her baby sister Pegge? But she seems curious and happy. She has just recently given up her own bottle; but when she sees the baby's bottle, she takes hold of it every chance she gets. There are those who attribute to this common occurrence of childhood the later desire to turn to the bottle for comfort when things get tough.

3 Years Apart

At the age of three, Bonnie is ready to understand a bit more about the birth of her little sister. There is real tenderness in her way of approaching the baby to give her a kiss.

3½ Years Apart

Johnny is three and a half. He has asked many questions during his mother's pregnancy and after little Debbie cane home. But he still looks puzzled sometimes. He has asked to stay home from nursery school. He would like to be with his mother and the baby all the time. His mother thinks that she will allow him to stay home and satisfy his curiosity for a few days. Then he will be ready to resume his independent activities.

4 Years Apart

Steven, four, has become not only excited, but excitable since the arrival of his sister Robin. He wants to show off and attract attention whenever his father plays with the baby.

5 Years Apart

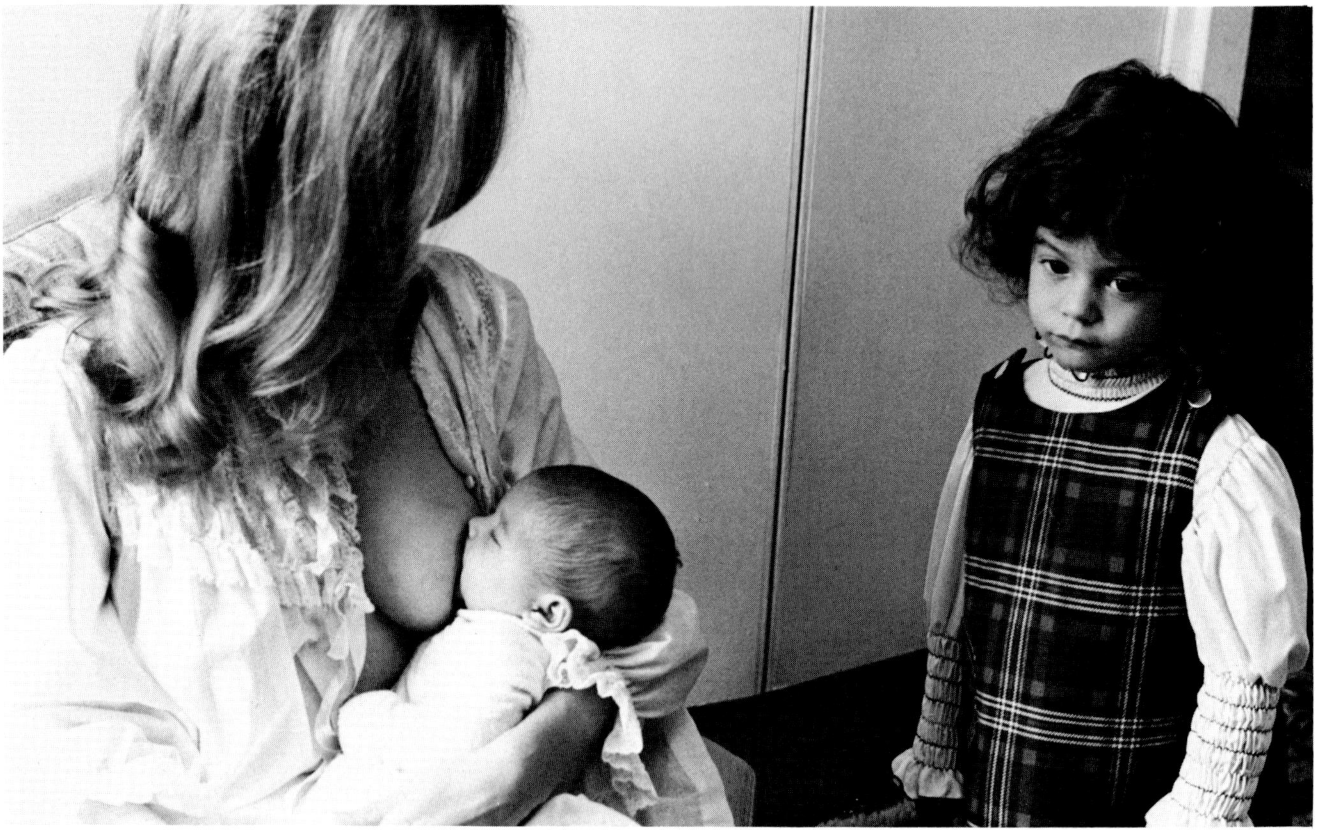

Joelle is five. She has become quieter since the birth of her baby sister. Feeding times seem endless to her—still she cannot decide to go and play by herself. Her parents make sure that she gets some time alone with them.

Children who are much older than their "kid brother or sister" tend to take on a quasi-parental role. They often form the buffer between the parents and the younger children and negotiate on behalf of the little ones. Sometimes they resent their ambiguous position, feeling put upon in a situation where they often act as parents without real authority but real problems nevertheless.

Eleven-year-old Kerry is once again comforting her four-year-old sister Kathy, who is scared of a lightning storm. Kerry has done her "Little Mother" job so well that all her siblings adore her. When Kerry recently got married, Cathy suggested, half in jest, that she would like to follow Kerry into her new home.

7 Years Apart

10 Years Apart

12 Years Apart

Jane is fifteen years old, her sister Rhoda three. There is a very special relationship between them, and Rhoda is used to having not only youthful, loving parents, but two older siblings as well. It is a lucky coincidence that by the time Jane will go off to college, Rhoda will be old enough to go to school and make new friends.

Darrell, ten and a half, is really enjoying playing mother. Her baby brother Talbot is more fun than any doll she ever had. And her mother appreciates the help she gets from Darrell.

9 and 11 Years Apart

Katherine and Heather are teenagers who are getting an early experience in the ways of small children. They have a little brother, Jonathan, five and a half. When he wants something, they find it hard to resist him. First he talks, then he hugs, and pretty soon they are doing what he wants them to do—in this case, go to the Adventure Playground in New York's Central Park and play with him on the swings, monkey bars, and slides.

Two Years Apart at Different Ages

The one year old wants to play peekaboo, the three year old insists on going outside: it can be pretty difficult to satisfy the wishes of children who are two years apart.

The same two-year difference hardly matters when eight-year-old Amelia and six-year-old Rebecca ask their mother to read a story to them.

Two Years Apart at Different Ages

The nearly two-year age difference between five-year-old Sandy and three-year-old Alison seems to vary from moment to moment. They experience many competitive, angry moments only to appear arm in arm, beaming at each other soon afterwards. Later in life, they grew so close that they decided to room together in boarding school—not exactly a common practice between siblings.

At about the time that the younger of the two sisters, Kim, started school, she and Wendy became best friends. Here they are six and eight years old. They are joined in concern for a sick bird they found in the garden.

Seven-year-old Chrissy and five-year-old Pegge have also reached a harmonious stage in their lives: they like to do many of the same things and are having lots of fun.

Can a parent do something about bridging the gap that separates two children at a given moment in their development? Matthew, six, has recently become very excited about doing quite difficult jigsaw puzzles. His four-year-old sister Sonya doesn't understand why her way of playing with the puzzles so upsets her brother. Matthew is usually very patient with Sonya; but when she grabs at pieces of his beloved puzzles or loses the pieces, he can hardly restrain himself from using his superior strength on her. The sounds of the battle bring Mother running. Should she use this opportunity to teach Sonya how to do a puzzle or just remove her from the scene? She compromises by sitting down to read one of Sonya's favorite stories, while Matthew can finish his puzzle with visible pleasure.

Whatever the age difference between children, there will always be times when a new phase of development propels the older one into another world, where the younger one cannot follow.

Eight-year-old Sally reads with great ease. Her five-year-old sister Jane has just become really interested in learning, too; she listens to her older sister in wonder and with some envy.

When One Child Is Ahead of the Other

Another situation in which a two-year age difference looms large. Three-year-old Ira can easily climb up on his parents' bed to work on his beloved puzzle in peace and quiet, while his one-year-old sister Molly can only stand there, full of frustration.

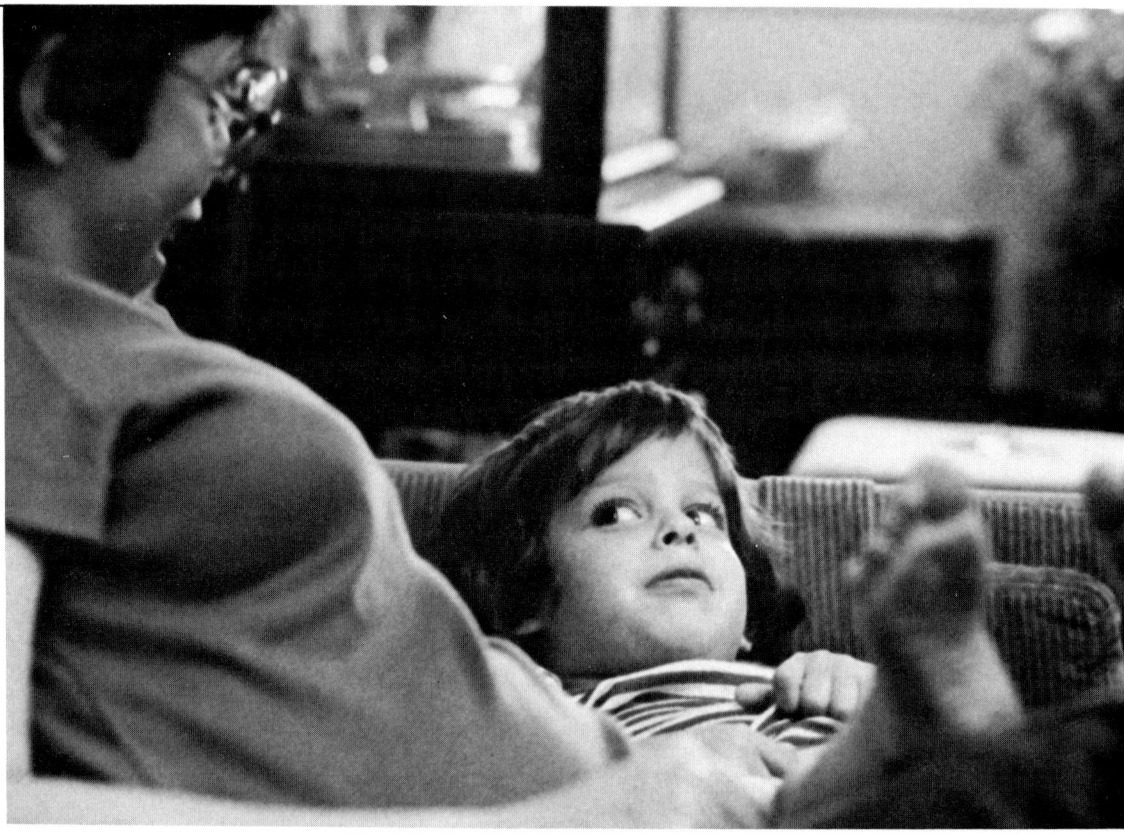

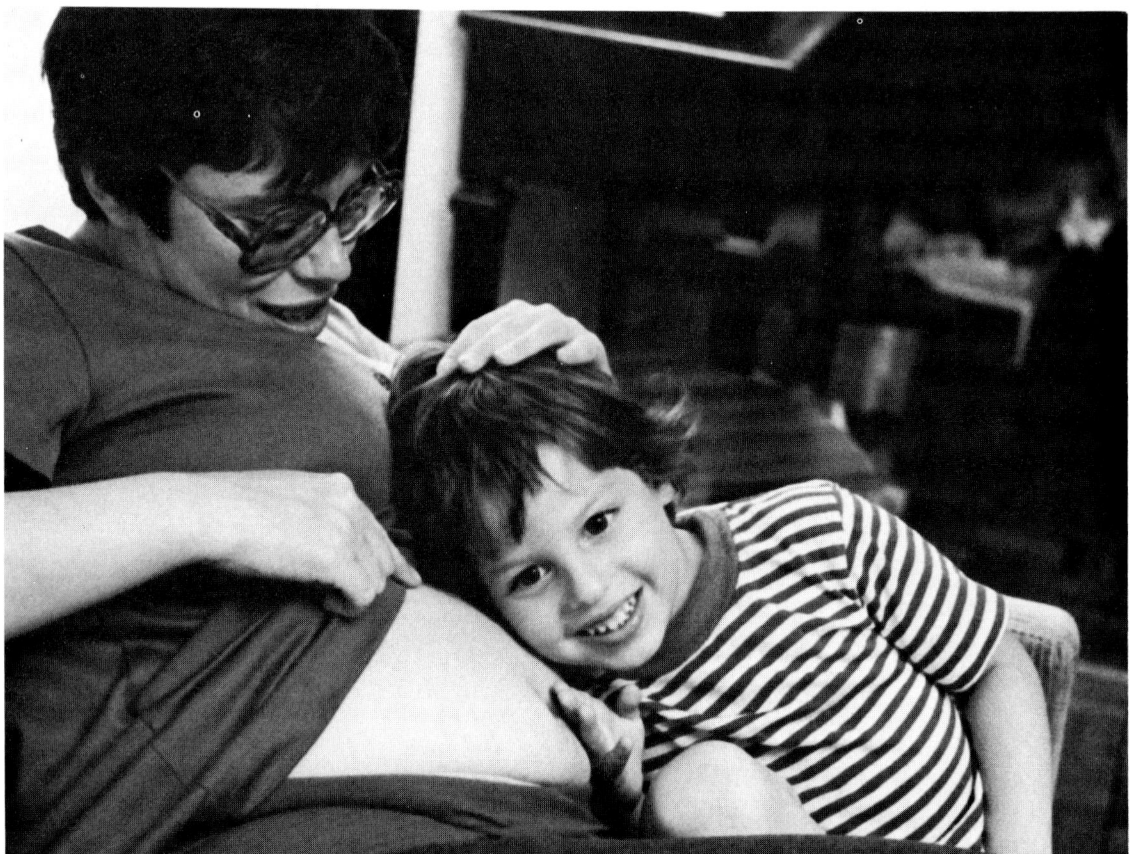

ARAM AND ZOE: A SPECIAL STORY

Zoe Taleporos was born on October 23, 1979, when her brother Aram was four years old. Suzanne took pictures of the Taleporos family from Betsy's pregnancy with Zoe through the first couple of years of Zoe's life.

When Aram was three, I became pregnant. I worried about how to break the news to him. Up to this point he was only mildly interested in babies. He did say once that he wanted a baby, but he also said that he wanted a cat. His reaction was encouraging. "Just what I ordered!" were his first words. Evidently, he wanted it to be his idea. But later, he wasn't so sure. "I think I'd really rather have a cat." I told him that it was going to be a baby, not a cat, and that this was an irreversible decision.

Naturally, Aram was curious about the new baby. Where would she sleep? What would she eat? Would she take away his toys? Would she like him? Would he like her?

Certain inevitable questions about conception and birth came up in the latter part of my pregnancy. Mostly he wanted to know about the baby inside of me. How did she breathe? Why didn't she drown? Could she hear? How was she going to get out?

We got some picture books that showed the baby growing inside the womb. We talked a bit about how you need a mommy and a daddy to make a baby. This seemed to satisfy Aram; he didn't probe beyond his capacity to understand and my capacity to explain.

Sometimes Aram tried to feel the baby moving around inside me, kicking or hiccuping. He alternated between playing at being big brother to being mother. Most of the time he went about his own business and got annoyed when I tired easily and didn't pick him up. I heard him explaining to a friend what it was like to be pregnant: "You get real fat and then you get real sick before the baby comes out."

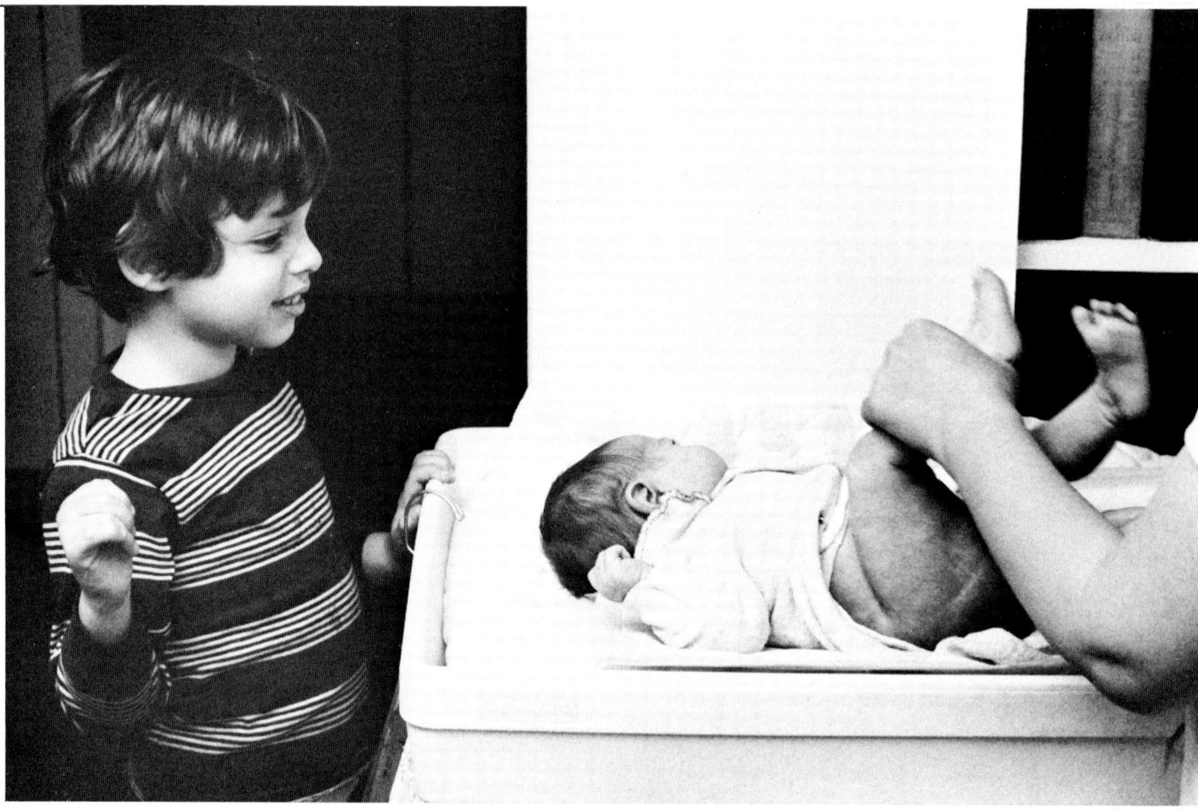

First Weeks

We spent a lot of time talking about Aram as a baby. We talked about all the things we had done for him as a baby; we showed him pictures of himself wearing some of the same clothes that Zoe was now wearing.

Aram was very interested in seeing Zoe's diapers being changed. We let him help until the fascination ebbed for him, in about a week or so.

He also had a babydoll of his own to take care of. While I fed Zoe, he fed his doll. He changed the doll, burped it, sang to it, and scolded it.

Sometimes Aram asked me whether he would still be as important to me as before, but basically it was an easy adjustment. I tried to let him say his piece without forcing him to express hostile and angry feelings. Parents may expect negative feelings so much that they put the idea in their child's mind before the child actually comes up with it himself.

There was no doubt, however, that we all had to adjust. We were a larger family now. And Aram was no longer an only child. His life had changed overnight—and the change was irreversible.

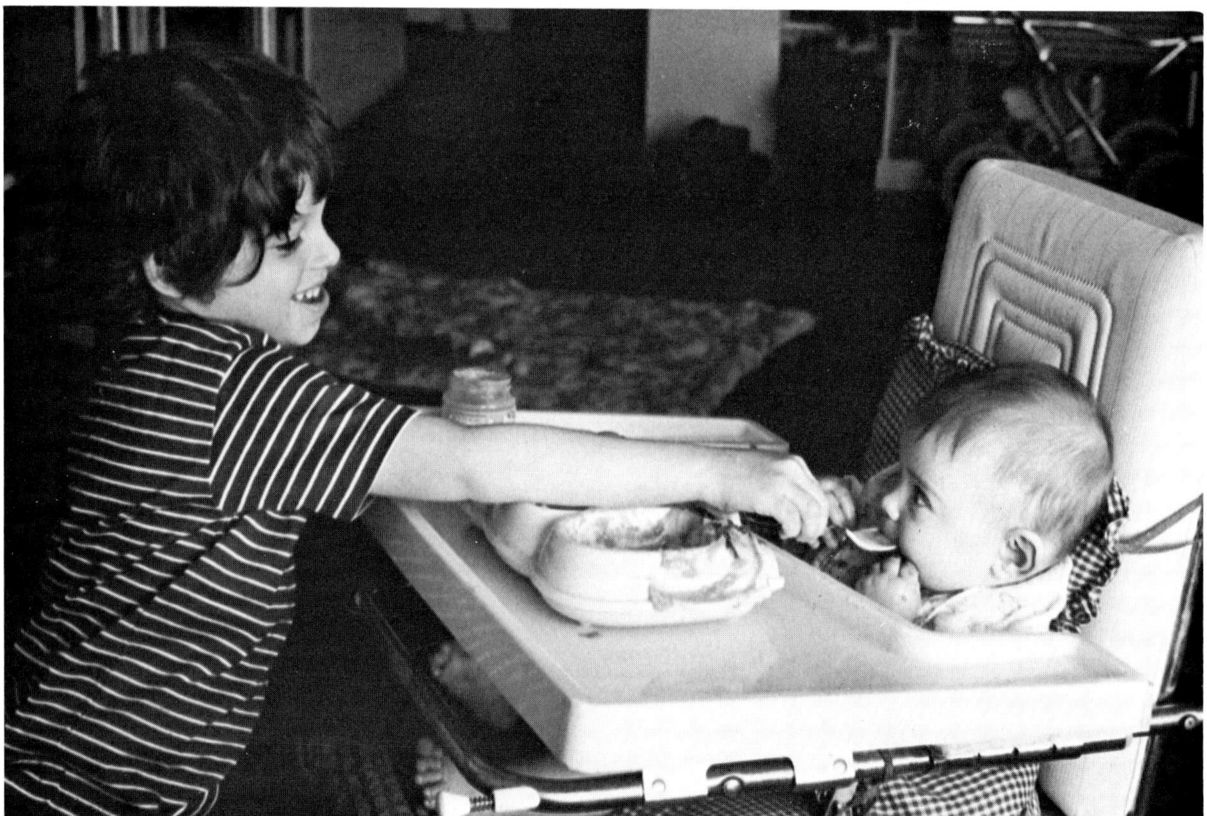

Aram Thinks Zoe Is Fun

As we settled in as a family, Zoe became an outgoing, adventurous baby. For an older brother, this is generally a golden time. Zoe was cute and funny, and Aram could play with her without her really getting in his way or into his toys.

A lot of their good times revolved around family routines. Mealtimes were especially fun. Zoe would sit in her highchair, watching us eat or asking to be fed. It was often quite messy. I let Aram help with the feedings as often as he wanted to. Zoe wasn't always sure she wanted Aram to feed her, but it turned into some of the closest times for them. It was terrific for me to have such a willing helper feed the baby while I finished cooking the rest of the family's dinner.

Zoe Becomes Independent

Bath time has always been one of the best times in our family routines. Aram and Zoe splashed and laughed and tickled each other. They invented all kinds of silly games. Aram often had to protect himself from Zoe's grabbing hands, although the uninhibited play delighted him.

Aram was especially patient with Zoe. His concerns about her hitting him or hurting him, expressed before she was born, didn't seem to be real as he got to know her. He let her tug at him, pull his hair, and explore his mouth with her little hands. Although I never felt that Zoe was ever strong enough to hurt Aram, I kept an eye on things.

Zoe managed to call the shots; if she wasn't in the mood to be held, or if she didn't feel secure in the way Aram was holding her, she let us know.

Having two children is certainly more difficult than having one. The actual caring doubled. In addition, we had to deal with each one individually. This seemed to be especially important for Aram at this point since he had been used to undivided attention.

Often, my husband and I split taking care of the children on weekends. I would take Aram out one day to do something with him that he especially wanted to do, and my husband would do the same on another day. That way, we had time to spend alone with our new baby, without feeling the pull of having to attend to the needs of two children at once.

Aram and Zoe Fight

As Zoe grew older, the children spent more time in real play. They had some of the same interests and toys. As their relationship grew, they began to share and give to each other in ways that are very hard for young children.

One of their first fights happened on the beach when Zoe took Aram's pail away from him. As with most of the fights that followed, Aram's reaction was to scream at her and to yell for help. Fortunately, he rarely became physically aggressive with her. At this stage it was usually Zoe who started the fighting. It was hard for her to understand that she shouldn't grab Aram's toys and hit when she wanted something. It took a long time for her to learn otherwise.

A Visit with Grandparents

Grandpa and Grandma were always very important to Aram. We are a close family, and they paid a lot of attention to him when his sister was born. There was always some extra-special treat to look forward to.

Later, Zoe joined Aram when visiting their grandparents. Each child developed different and separate relationships with them. I usually found the children happy and excited—if somewhat exhausted—when I came to pick them up. One day, Aram greeted me by showing me a tooth that had become loose. Zoe decided that her tooth was loose, too, and kept showing it off in her effort to keep up with big brother.

Birthdays

When Zoe's first birthday arrived, we all breathed a sigh of relief as we realized that we had finally made it through this critical time. As we sat down to celebrate, we felt that our sense of being a family had enlarged—that we had become used to being four instead of three.

True to her fearless ways, Zoe reached out to touch the candle on her first cake. We all ended up comforting her as she learned her first lesson about fire. Aram was the proud big brother helping to blow out the candles once they were relit.

By her second birthday, Zoe had learned a lot. She had grown very assertive. While she didn't touch the candles again, she insisted on doing everything else by herself. In fact she cried each time the candles were blown out, wanting to start it all over again.

As I watched my children play during Zoe's second birthday party, I realized how much had changed in their lives over the past two years. They seemed to spark each other with gaiety and laughter. The fights were more frequent and more serious, as Aram and Zoe began to compete more. But the play had become serious, too. At first each one did his or her own thing in the same room. But by the time Zoe turned three, they had begun to play make-believe games that called for true give and take. Their need for adult supervision in their play grew less and less as their play became more satisfying and Aram and Zoe became surer of each other as playmates.